Striking Emptiness

Zen Master Dogen's *Bendōwa*

Striking Emptiness

Zen Master Dogen's *Bendōwa*

Commentary by

Daniel Kōjin Gallagher

Foreword by David keizan Scott Roshi

Translated by Norman Waddell and Masao Abe

Hope Street Press

Naples & Liverpool

Striking Emptiness:

Zen Master Dogen's *Bendōwa*

Copyright © 2024 Daniel Kōjin Gallagher

All rights reserved.

First edition December 2024

Cover art: Maruyama Okyo, Mount Fuji

Cover design: German Creative

ISBN: 979-8-9915155-0-4

Hope Street Press

This commentary is dedicated to:
Sunyana Graef Roshi of the Vermont Zen Center.

The sound that issues from the striking of emptiness is an endless and wondrous voice that resounds before and after the fall of the hammer.

— Eihei Dogen

Contents

Acknowledgements

I am deeply indebted to Dr. David Keizan Scott Roshi, founder of StoneWater Zen Sangha in Liverpool, England. His steadfast encouragement and thoughtful comments were vital to the development and completion of this work.

Sarah Kokai Thwaites was an indispensable reader, advisor, and friend during the arduous editing process. Sarah meticulously read the entire manuscript and her keen insights and constructive feedback were invaluable to me.

Hank Yoshin Malinowski Sensei offered me frank and sincere advice on crucial aspects of this work, without which this book would look vastly different.

John Tarrant Roshi of the Pacific Zen Institute was an inspiration while I was working on this manuscript.

My sincere gratitude extends to Catherine Genno Pagès Roshi for many years of training and her ever-present and benevolent influence.

Grateful acknowledgement is given to the New York Metropolitan Museum of Art for permission to reprint Maruyama Okyo's 18th century painting, "Mount Fuji" on the cover.

Finally, I wish to acknowledge my profound gratitude to the Eastern Buddhist Society of Kyoto, Japan, for their generous support in granting us permission to reprint Masao Abe and Norman Waddell's translation of the *Bendōwa*.

Foreword

Striking Emptiness: Zen Master Dogen's Bendowa, is the culmination of years of study, practice, and reflection. Dogen's *Bendowa* is a seminal work in Zen literature, offering profound clarity into the nature of Zen practice and enlightenment. Through his insightful and heartfelt commentary, Daniel Kōjin Gallagher provides readers with a way into Dogen's teachings, illuminating their relevance for contemporary folk.

This commentary is not an academic endeavor but a living, breathing testament to the transformative power of Zen. It reflects the same dedication and depth that Kōjin has brought to his own practise and to his engagement with the Zen community over the years. His commentary is rooted in a clear understanding of Zen that has been honed through decades of personal experience and dedicated meditation.

In addition to his work on the *Bendowa*, Kōjin has previously explored Dogen's writing in his first book, *Meeting the True Dragon*, a thoughtful examination of Dogen's *Fukanzazengi*. This text laid a solid foundation for his understanding and appreciation of Zen practise, enriching his approach to Dogen's work and further demonstrating his ability to make Dogen more accessible to everyday folk.

Kōjin earned a PhD in Comparative Literature from the University of Paris, while teaching full time at the university and living at Dana Zen Center in Montreuil where he practised for many years under the guidance of the venerable Catherine Genno Pagès Roshi. His rigorous academic work and sincere dedication to his Zen practice bring a rich and informed perspective to his commentary on the *Bendowa*.

As you embark on this journey through *Striking Emptiness*, I invite you to approach this text with an open mind and a receptive heart, much in the same way that we approach our Zen practise. May this book serve as a guide and inspiration, offering folk a deeper appreciation of Dogen's timeless wisdom and its application in our lives today.

Keizan Scott Roshi
Liverpool

Introduction[1]

On a warm and humid late summer morning, on the outskirts of the southern district of Kyoto known as Fukakusa, a young Buddhist monk named Kigen Dogen sat down with a brush and an inkwell. Having just finished tidying up his quarters after morning meditation and a simple meal of rice and pickles, he settled onto the tatami mat, unrolled a sheet of rice paper, and began to write a short treatise in praise of zazen and the Zen Buddhist spiritual path. The year was 1231, and he titled the essay *Bendōwa* — "On the Endeavor of the Way."

At 31 years old, Dogen was already deeply immersed in his spiritual journey.

[1] The background on Dogen's life contained in this introduction was inspired by the introduction of *Meeting the True Dragon: Zen Master Dogen's Fukanzazengi.*

Born in Kyoto in 1200, Eihei Dogen's early life remains somewhat obscure. The sole biography of him was written in the 15th century and remained unpublished for centuries. According to legend, he was born into an aristocratic family and displayed intelligence from a young age. Raised in the Tendai school of Buddhism, which held significant political and popular sway in Japan, Dogen experienced his first spiritual awakening at the tender age of seven during his mother's funeral. Witnessing smoke rise from an incense stick, he grasped the impermanence of life. The loss of both parents — his father five years earlier and his mother more recently — had a profound impact on him.

At 12, Dogen was ordained in the Tendai school and resided at Enraku Temple on Mount Hiei. He later moved to Kennin Temple, Japan's first Zen monastery, founded in 1202, which blended elements of various Buddhist traditions despite its Zen focus. Dogen spent nine formative years at Kennin Temple studying under Butsuju Myozen (1184 - 1225), from whom he received Rinzai Transmission in the Oryx lineage. In 1223, Myozen embarked on a pilgrimage to China and invited Dogen to accompany him. They traveled extensively, visiting numerous monasteries until settling at Tainting Monastery.

In the *Bendōwa* Dogen wrote:

> Then, when I returned home, in the first year of the She-ting period of the Sung [1228], my

thoughts immediately turned to preaching the Dharma[2] for the salvation of my fellow beings — it was as though I had taken a heavy burden upon my shoulders. Nevertheless, in order to await the time when I can work vigorously to this end and unburden myself of the desire to spread the Dharma far and wide, I am for the time being living like a cloud or water plant, drifting without any fixed abode, attempting to transmit through my actions the way of life followed by outstanding Zen masters of the past.

When Dogen sat down to write Bendōwa in 1231, he had only returned to Japan four years earlier from a transformative five-year journey to China. Upon his return, he spent most of his time at Kennin temple in Kyoto. However, Dogen found the training at Kennin less rigorous and grew disinterested in the non-Zen rituals and services. Determined to follow his own path and transmit the teachings he had received in China, Dogen left Kennin and journeyed south until he discovered a dilapidated temple suitable for his practice and writing.

Apart from his personal reasons for leaving Kennin Temple, historical accounts suggest that Dogen was compelled to depart by the Tendai sect of Mount Hiei. In a surviving letter addressed to the poet Fujiwara Taika (1162 - 1241), Dogen details how the Hiei priesthood contemplated demolishing his dwelling and expelling him from the capital. Amidst these tumultuous

---

[2] Here "Dharma" refers to the teaching of the Buddha.

circumstances, Dogen sought refuge in a small temple on the southern outskirts of Kyoto, where he could practice and write in peace and safety.

Soon after, monks began arriving at Dogen's temple to train with him, the community grew in size. Dogen eventually moved into a nearby building called Kannondoriin, located on the grounds of the deteriorating Gokuraku temple. In 1243, he founded Eihei temple about 100 miles north in a rural, mountainous region of Fukui prefecture.

Following Dogen's death in 1253, the *Bendōwa* fell into obscurity, known only to a small number of Soto priests. It remained largely forgotten for nearly 450 years until it was rediscovered during the Kambun period (1661-1673) of the Tokugawa era. Although the exact circumstances of its rediscovery are uncertain, a popular account suggests it was found in the residence of a noble family in Kyoto. In 1684, the *Bendōwa* was included in the *Shōbōgenzō*, a collection gathered and published by the priest Manzan Dohaku. Over a century later, in 1788, Eihei temple published the *Bendōwa* in a single volume.

In 1926, Doshu Okubo discovered a copy of the *Bendōwa* in the archives of Shobo temple in Iwata prefecture. This version, dated 1515, was based on a 1332 manuscript copy and differed slightly from the well-known version of the *Bendōwa*. For instance, it contained 19 questions and answers instead of the standard 18.

Bendōwa can be divided into two distinct sections. The first part, constituting roughly a quarter of the entire text, is where Dogen expounds on the virtues of zazen and the power of jijuyu samadhi. Here, he traces the lineage of the mind seal — from Shakyamuni Buddha through the renowned Chinese Zen masters — and shares personal anecdotes of his pilgrimage to China. This section stands as the heart of the *Bendōwa*, showcasing Dogen at his most eloquent and powerful.

The remaining three-quarters of the text comprises the second part, featuring a series of 18 questions and answers. These questions, posed by an unidentified individual, likely compile inquiries Dogen received from various disciples rather than representing the queries of a single person.

Ultimately, *Bendōwa* serves as a spiritual guide, intended to inspire students on their path to awakening to their true nature. It reflects Dogen's profound enlightenment and his passionate commitment to guiding others along the Way.

Bendōwa

Buddha-tathagatas all have a wonderful means, unexcelled and free from human agency, for transmitting the wondrous Dharma and realizing supreme and complete awakening. That this means is only passed directly from Buddha to Buddha without deviation is due to the jijuyu samadhi, which is its touchstone.

To disport oneself freely in this samadhi, the right entrance is proper sitting in zazen. The Dharma is amply present in every person, but without practice, it is not manifested; without realization, it is not attained. It is not a question of one or many; let loose of it and it fills your hands. It is not bounded vertically or horizontally; speak it and it fills your mouth. Within this Dharma, Buddhas dwell everlastingly, leaving no perceptions in any sphere or direction; all living beings use it unceasingly, with no sphere or direction appearing in their perceptions.

The negotiation of the Way with concentrated effort that I now teach makes myriad dharmas exist in realization and, in transcending realization, practices a total reality. Then, when you are over the barrier, with all bonds cast off, you are no longer affected by such segmented distinctions."

After the religious mind arose in me, awakening the desire to seek the Way, I visited many religious teachers throughout the country. I chanced to encounter the priest Myozen of Kennin-ji. Swiftly passed the frosts and flowers of the nine years I studied with him. During that time I learned something of the manner of the Rinzai school. As the chief disciple of the patriarch Eisai, it was Myozen alone who genuinely transmitted the supreme Buddha Dharma. None of Eisai's other followers could compare with him.

After that, I proceeded to great Sung China, where I visited leading priests of the Liang-che region and learned of the characteristics of the Five Zen Gates. Finally, I practiced under Zen master Ju-ching at Mount T'ai-pai, and there I resolved the one great matter of Zen practice for my entire life. Then, when I returned home, in the first year of the She-ting period of the Sung [1228], my thoughts immediately turned to preaching the Dharma for the salvation of my fellow beings — it was as though I had taken a heavy burden upon my shoulders. Nevertheless, in order to await the time when I can work vigorously to this end and unburden myself of the desire to spread the Dharma far and wide, I am for the time being living like a cloud or water plant, drifting without any fixed abode, attempting to transmit through my actions the way of life followed by outstanding Zen masters of the past.

But there will be those who have no concern for gain or glory, authentic religious seekers whose desire for the Way takes precedence over all else. They will be led vainly astray by mistaken teachers, and the right understanding will be arbitrarily obscured from them. They will become needlessly drunk with their own delusions and immersed forever in the world of illusion. How can the true seed of prajna *be expected to quicken and grow within such seekers? How will they ever reach the moment of attainment? As I am now committed to a wandering life, to what mountain or river can they proceed to find me? It is a sense of pity for the plight of such people that now makes me write down for those who would learn to practice the Way, the customs and standards of the Zen monasteries of great Sung China that I saw with [my] own eyes and have learned and the profound teachings of their masters that I have succeeded to and follow and transmit. I want such seekers to know the right Buddha Dharma. Here are its true essentials.*

At an assembly on Vulture Peak, the great teacher Shakyamuni Buddha imparted to Mahakashyapa the Dharma that was subsequently transmitted from patriarch to patriarch down to Bodhidharma. Bodhidharma traveled to China and conveyed the Dharma to Hui-k'e, marking the initial transmission of the Buddha Dharma to eastern lands. It then made its way in direct, personal transmission to the Sixth Patriarch, Ta-chien. By that time, the genuine Buddha Dharma had beyond doubt spread extensively in China. It appeared there with its essence unaffected by any ramifying doctrinal accretions. The Sixth Patriarch had two superior disciples, Huai-jang of Nan-yüeh and Hsing-ssu of Ch'ing-ün. As possessors and transmitters of the Buddha-seal, they were masters for men and devas alike. Their two schools spread and branched into Five Houses: the Fa-yen, Kwei-yang, Ts'ao-tung, Yün-men and Lin-chi schools. At present in the great Sung, the Lin-chi school alone is found throughout the country. Although among these Five Houses there are differences to be found, they are all equally based on the one Buddha-mind seal.

Scriptural writings were transmitted to China from the western lands during the Latter Han dynasty. They spread over the empire. But even in China, no determination was reached about which of the various teachings was superior. Following the arrival of Bodhidharma from the west, these entangling complications were cut away at their source, and the one Buddha Dharma, free from all impurity, began to spread. We must pray that this will take place in our country as well.

It is said that all the patriarchs and Buddhas who have maintained the Buddha Dharma have without question considered practice based upon proper sitting in jijuyu samadhi as the right path that led to their enlightenment. All those who have gained enlightenment in India and China have followed in this way of practice as well. It is a matter of rightly transmitting the wonderful means in personal encounter from master to disciple, and on the disciple's sustaining the true essence thus received.

According to the authentic tradition of Buddhism, this personally and directly transmitted Buddha Dharma is the supreme of the supreme. From the first time you go before your master and receive his teaching, you no longer have need for incise-offerings, homage-paying, nembutsu, penance disciplines, or sutra reading. Just cast off your body and mind in the practice of zazen.

When even for a short period of time you sit properly in samadhi, imprinting the Buddha-seal in your three activities of deed, word and thought, then each and every thing throughout the dharma world is the Buddha-seal, and all space without exception is enlightenment. Accordingly, it makes Buddhatathagatas increase the Dharma-joy welling from their original source and renews the adornments of the Way of enlightenment. Then, when all classes of all beings in the ten directions of the universe — hell-dwellers, craving spirits, and animals; fighting demons, humans, and devas — being all together emancipation and reveal their original aspects, at that time all things together realize in themselves the true enlightenment of the Buddhas. Utilizing the Buddha-body and immediately leaping beyond the confines of this personal enlightenment, they sit erect beneath the kingly tree of enlightenment, turn simultaneously the great and utterly incomparable Dharma wheel, and expound the ultimate and profound prajna *free from all human agency.*

Since, moreover, these enlightened ones in their turn enter directly into the way of imperceptible mutual assistance, the person seated in zazen without fail casts off body and mind, severs all the heretofore disordered and defiled thoughts and views emanating from his discriminating consciousness, conforms totally with the genuine Buddha Dharma, and assists universally in performing Buddha-work far and wide, at each of the various places the Buddha-tathagatas teach, that are as infinitely numberless as the smallest atom particles — imparting universally the ki *transcending Buddha, vigorously promoting the Dharma* (ho) *transcending Buddha. Then, with land, trees and grasses, fence and wall, tile and pebble, and all the things in the ten directions performing the work of Buddhas, the persons who share in the benefits thus produced from this wind and water all are imparted unperceived the wonderful and incomprehensible teaching and guidance of the Buddhas, and all manifest their own immediate and familiar enlightenment close at hand. Since those receiving and employing this fire and water all turn round and round the Buddha-making activity of original enlightenment, those who dwell and converse with them also join with one another in possessing inexhaustible Buddha-virtue, spreading it ever wider, circulating the inexhaustible, unceasing, incomprehensible, and immeasurable Buddha Dharma inside and outside throughout the universe.*

Yet such things are not mingled in the perceptions of the person sitting in zazen because, occurring in the stillness of samadhi beyond human agency or artifact, they are, directly and immediately, realization. If practice and realization were two different stages, as ordinary people consider them to be, they should perceive each other. Any such mingling with perceptions is not the mark of realization, for the mark of true realization is to be altogether beyond such illusion.

Moreover, although both the mind of the person seated in zazen and its environment enter realization and leave realization within the stillness of samadhi, as it occurs in the sphere of jijuyu, it does not disturb a single mote of dust, or obstruct a single phenomenon, but performs great and wide-ranging Buddha-work and carries on the exceedingly profound, recondite activities of preaching and enlightening. The trees, grasses, and land involved in this all emit a bright and shining light, preaching the profound and incomprehensible Dharma; and it is endless. Trees and grasses, wall and fence expound and exalt the Dharma for the sake of ordinary people, sages, and all living beings. Ordinary people, sages, and all living beings in turn preach and exalt the Dharma for the sake of trees, grasses, wall and fence. The realm of self-enlightenment qua *enlightening others is originally filled with the characteristics of realization with no lack whatsoever, and the ways of realization continue on unceasingly.*

Because of this, when just one person does zazen even one time, he becomes, imperceptibly, one with each and all of the myriad things and permeates completely all time, so that within the limitless universe, throughout past, future, and present, he is performing the eternal and ceaseless work of guiding beings to enlightenment. It is, for each and every thing, one and the same undifferentiated practice, one and the same undifferentiated realization. Only this is not limited to practice of sitting alone: the sound that issues from the striking of emptiness is an endless and wondrous voice that resounds before and after the fall of the hammer. And this is not limited to the side of the practicer alone. Each and every thing is, in its original aspect, endowed with original practice—it cannot be measured or comprehended. You must understand that even if all the numberless Buddhas in the ten directions, as countless as the sands of the Ganges, mustered all their might together and by means of Buddha-wisdom attempted to measure and totally know the merit of the zazen of a single person, they could not know the whole of its measure.

[QUESTIONS AND ANSWERS]

Question 1: You have told us all about the sublime merits of zazen. But an ordinary person might ask you this: "There are many entrances to the Buddha Dharma. What is it that makes you advocate zazen alone?"

Answer 1: Because it is the right entrance to the Buddha Dharma.

Question 2: But why single out zazen alone as the right entrance?

Answer 2: The great teacher Shakyamuni Buddha rightly transmitted zazen as the wonderful means for attaining the Way; all the tathagatas of the three periods attain the Way through zazen as well — which is why they transmit it from one to another as the true entrance. Besides, zazen is how all patriarchs from India in the west to China in the east, have gained the Way. That is why I now teach it to men and devas as the right entrance.

Question 3: The reason you give, that zazen transmits the Tathagata's wonderful means, which you base upon evidence you trace to the patriarchal teachers, may well be correct — such matters are really beyond an ordinary person's ability to ascertain. For all that, however, surely one can reach enlightenment by reciting sutras and repeating the nembutsu. How can you be certain that if you pass your time sitting idly in zazen, enlightenment will result?

Answer 3: When you characterize the unsurprisingly great Dharma and the samadhi of the Buddhas as merely "sitting idly," you are guilty of maligning the Great Vehicle. It is as profound an illusion as to declare there is no water when you are sitting in the midst of the ocean. Fortunately, the Buddhas are already seated firmly established in jijuyu samadhi. Does that not produce immense merit? It is a pity that your eyes are not opened yet, that intoxication still befogs your mind.

The realm of Buddhas is utterly incomprehensible, not to be reached by the workings of the mind. How could it ever be known to a man of disbelief or inferior intelligence? Only a person of great capacity and true faith is able to enter here. A person who does not believe, even if he is told about such a realm, will find it impossible to comprehend. Even on Vulture Peak, the Buddha told some in the assembly that they might leave. If right faith arises in your mind, you should practice under a master. If it does not, you should cease your efforts for the time being and reflect with regret that you have not been favored with Dharma benefits from the past.

Besides, what do you really know of the merits brought by such practices as sutra-recitation and nembutsu? It is utterly futile to imagine that merely moving your tongue or raising your voice has the merit of Buddha-work. Any attempt to equate those practices with the Buddha Dharma only makes it more remote. Moreover, when you open a sutra to read, it should be

17

for the purpose of clarifying the teachings the Buddha set forth about the rules and regulations for practicing sudden and gradual enlightenment, to convince you that you will attain realization if you follow them. It is not done in order to waste yourself in useless speculation and discrimination, and to suppose that you are thereby gaining merit that will bring you to enlightenment. Intending to attain the Buddha Way by foolishly working your lips, repeating some words incessantly a thousand or ten thousand times, is like pointing the thills of a cart northward when you want to go south, or like trying to fit a square piece of wood into a round hole. To read the Buddha's words while still unaware of the way of practice is as worthless a pastime as perusing a medical prescription and overlooking to mix the compounds for it. If you merely raise your voice in endless recitation, you are in no way different from a frog in a spring field — although you croak from morning to nightfall, it will bring you no benefit at all. Such practices are difficult to relinquish for those who are deeply deluded by fame or profit — this because of the depth of their covetousness. Such people were to be found in ancient times; there is no reason they should not be around today. They deserve our special pity.

Only make no mistake about this: if a student working under the constant guidance of a clear-minded, truly enlightened teacher realizes his original mind and rightly transmits his Dharma, the wondrous Dharma of the Seven Buddhas is then fully manifested and fully maintained. There is no way for this to be known or even to be approached by a priest who merely studies words. So you should have done with all these uncertainties and illusions; instead, negotiate the Way in zazen under the guidance of a true teacher and gain complete realization of the Buddhas' jijuyu samadhi.

Question 4: The teachings that are transmitted today in our own Hokke and Kegon schools represent the ultimate Mahayana teaching. Not to mention the teachings of Shingon, which were transmitted personally by Vairochana Buddha to Vajrasattva — they have not been handed down from master to disciple without good reason. Centered in the sayings "the mind in itself is Buddha," and "this very mind attains Buddhahood," Shingon teaches that the genuine enlightenment of the Five Buddhas is attainable in a single sitting, without having to pass through long kalpas of religious practice. It could perhaps be termed the most sublime point the Buddha Dharma has yet reached. In view of that, What are the advantages of the practice you advocate that you advance it alone and ignore all these others?

Answer 4: Be well assured that for a Buddhist the issue is not to debate the superiority or inferiority of one teaching or another, or to establish their respective depths. All he needs to know is whether the practice is authentic or not. Men have flowed into the Way drawn by grasses and flowers, mountains and running water. They have received the lasting impression of the Buddha-seal by holding soil, rocks, sand, and pebbles. Indeed, its vast and great signature is imprinted on all the things in nature, and even then remains in great abundance. A single mote of dust suffices to turn the great Dharma wheel. Because of this, words like "the mind in itself is Buddha" are no more than the moon reflected on the water. The meaning of "sitting itself is attainment of Buddhahood" is a reflection in a *mirror. Do not get caught up in skillfully turned words and phrases. In encouraging you now to practice the immediate realization of enlightenment, I am showing you the wondrous Way by which the Buddha-patriarchs transmit the Dharma from one to another. I do this in the hope that you will become real men of the Way.*

Moreover, in receiving and transmitting the Buddha Dharma, it is absolutely essential to have as a teacher a person who is stamped with realization. Word-counting scholars will not do — that would be a case of the blind leading the blind. Today, all who follow the right transmission of the Buddha-patriarchs preserve and maintain the Buddha Dharma by following with reverence a clear-sighted master who has attained the Way and is in accord with realization. Because of that, the spirits of the realms of light and darkness come to him and take refuge; enlightened Arhats also seek him out to beg his teaching. None are excluded from acquiring the means of illuminating the mind-ground. This is something unheard of in other teachings. Followers of Buddha should simply learn the Buddha Dharma.

You should also know that basically we lack nothing of highest enlightenment. We are fully furnished with it at all times. But because we are unable to come to complete agreement with it, we learn to give rise to random intellection and, by chasing them, supposing them to be real, we stumble vainly in the midst of the great Way. From these mistaken views appear flowers in the air of various kinds: thoughts of a twelve-link chain of transmigration, realms of twenty-five forms of existence, notions of three vehicles, five vehicles, Buddha, no-

Buddha — they are endless. You must not think that learning such notions is the proper path of Buddhist practice.

But now, when you cast everything aside by single-mindedly performing zazen in exact accordance with the Buddha-seal, at that moment you outstep the confines of illusion and enlightenment, sentiment and calculation and, unbothered by alternatives of unenlightened and enlightened, you stroll at ease beyond the world of forms and regulations enjoying the function of great enlightenment. How can those enmeshed in the traps and snares of words and letters begin to measure up to you?

Question 5: Samadhi is one of the three learnings. Dhyana is one of the six paramitas.[3] Both are learned by all Bodhisattvas from the beginning of their religious life and practiced irrespective of a person's mental capacity. The zazen you speak of would seem to be included in these categories. What grounds do you have for stating that the right Dharma of the Buddha is concentrated solely in zazen?

Answer 5: Your question arises because the incomparable truth of the right Dharma eye that is the Buddha's great and central concern has come to be called the "Zen sect." Bear this well in mind: the appellation "Zen sect" is found in China and the lands east of China; it was unknown in India. During the nine years that the great teacher Bodhidharma performed zazen

---

3 The six "perfections" or *paramitas,* are practices which lead to the attainment of enlightenment: donation, precept-keeping, perseverance, assiduity, meditation, and wisdom.

facing a wall at the Shaolin monastery on Mount Sung, the priests and laymen of the time did not yet know the right Dharma of the Buddha. They said Bodhidharma was an Indian monk whose religion consisted of doing zazen. In generations after that all Buddhist patriarchs invariably devoted themselves to zazen. Unthinking people outside of the priesthood, observing this and not knowing the true circumstances, began to speak loosely of a "Zazen sect." At present, the word za has been dropped, and people speak of the Zen sect. The essence of the school is made clear throughout the recorded sayings of the Zen patriarchs. It is not to be equated with the samadhi or dhyana included among the six paramitas or three learnings.

Never has there been anything unclear or ambiguous about it. The Buddha himself wanted this Dharma to be his legitimate transmission. Some among the deva multitude now present in the heavens actually witnessed the ceremony that took place many years ago during the assembly on Vulture Peak, when the Tathagata [the Buddha] entrusted his right Dharma eye, his wondrous mind of nirvana, to Mahakashyapa alone. So there is no reason for any doubt. Without ever ceasing or diminishing their efforts, those deva hosts devote themselves to protecting and maintaining the Buddha Dharma throughout all eternity.

You should just know without any doubt or uncertainty whatever that this Dharma [zazen] is, in its entirety, the all-inclusive Way of the Buddha's Dharma. There is nothing else even to compare with it.

Question 6: What grounds are there for Buddhists to emphasize Zen meditation and place so much weight on sitting alone among the four attitudes (moving, standing, sitting, lying)? To say this is the path to entering realization?

Answer 6: It is not possible to exhaustively survey the way in which Buddhas, one after another from ages past, have practiced and entered realization. If you must have a reason, you should simply know that this is the way that Buddhists use. Further reasons are unnecessary. Haven't patriarchs extolled zazen as the "Dharma gate of repose and joy," because among the four bodily attitudes it is sitting that affords repose and joy? Remember, this is the way of practice employed not by one Buddha or two, but by all Buddhas and all patriarchs.

Question 7: So those who have not yet realized the Buddha Dharma can, by negotiating the Way in the practice of zazen, attain that realization. But what about those who have already achieved realization — what can they expect to gain by doing zazen?

Answer 7: Proverbs caution against relating one's dreams to the foolish, or placing boat-poles in the hands of woodsmen. Nevertheless, I will try to explain matters once again.

To think practice and realization are not one is a non-Buddhist view. In the Buddha Dharma, practice and realization are one and the same. As your present practice is practice within realization, your initial negotiation of the Way is in itself the whole of original realization. That is why from the time you are instructed in the way of practice, you are told not to anticipate realization apart from practice. It is because practice points directly to original realization. As it is from the very first realization in practice, realization is endless. As it is the practice of realization, practice is beginningless. Hence both Shakyamuni and Mahakashyapa were brought into the great functioning by practice within realization. Bodhidharma and patriarch Hui-neng were also drawn into the functioning by practice within realization. And it has been the same for all those who have maintained the Buddha's Dharma.

It is practice inseparable from the outset from realization, and since fortunately we [practicers] all transmit a portion of wondrous practice ourselves, even our negotiation of the Way as beginners obtains a portion of original realization at a ground that is utterly free of human agency. You should know that in order to keep from defiling this realization that is inseparable from practice Buddhas and patriarchs teach unceasingly that we must not allow our practice to diminish. When we cast off the wondrous practice, original realization fills our hands ; when we transcend original realization, wondrous practice permeates our bodies.

When I was in Sung China, everywhere I went I saw that the Zen monasteries were all built to include a special hall for zazen. Five hundred or 600 monks, sometimes even up to 2,000 monks, were housed in these halls and encouraged to devote themselves to zazen day and night. When I asked the head priests of these monasteries, teachers who transmit the authentic seal of the Buddha-mind, about the essence of the Buddha's Dharma, they told me that practice and realization are not two stages.

For that reason, I urge not only those who come here to practice with me, but all high-minded seekers who aspire to the truth that is found in the Buddha Dharma—whether beginners or experienced practicers, wise sages or just ordinary people—to conform to the teachings of the Buddha-patriarchs, to follow the Way of the true masters, and negotiate the Way in zazen.

Do you know the words of one of those patriarchs? "It is not that there is no practice or realization, only that we must not contaminate them [by attaching to them]." Another said: "Those who are able to see the Way, practice the Way." What you must understand is that your practice takes place within realization.

Question 8: In former times, when teachers traveled to China and returned as Dharma-transmitters to spread Buddhism in our country, why did they ignore zazen and transmit only the doctrines?

Answer 8: Teachers in the past did not transmit zazen because the circumstances were not yet ripe for it.

Question 9: Did the teachers of earlier times understand this Dharma (zazen)?

Answer 9: If they had, they would have made it known.

Question 10: Some have said: "Do not concern yourself about birth-and-death. There is a way to promptly rid yourself of birth-and-death. It is by grasping the reason for the eternal immutability of the 'mind-nature.' The gist of it is this: although once the body is born it proceeds inevitably to death, the mind-nature never perishes. Once you can realize that the mind-nature, which does not transmigrate in birth-and-death, exists in your own body, you make it your fundamental nature. Hence the body, being only a temporary form, dies here and is reborn there without end, yet the mind is immutable, unchanging throughout past, present, and future. To know this is to be free from birth-and-death. By realizing this truth, you put a final end to the transmigratory cycle in which you have been turning. When your body dies, you enter the ocean of the original nature. When you return to your origin in this ocean, you become endowed with the wondrous virtue of the Buddha-patriarchs. But even if you are able to grasp this in your present life, because your present physical existence embodies erroneous karma from prior lives, you are not the same as the sages.

"Those who fail to grasp this truth are destined to turn forever in the cycle of birth-and-death. What is necessary, then, is simply to know without delay the meaning of the mind-nature's immutability. What can you expect to gain from idling your entire life away in purposeless sitting?"

What do you think of this statement? Is it essentially in accord with the Way of the Buddhas and patriarchs?

Answer 10: You have just expounded the view of the Senika heresy. It is certainly not the Buddha Dharma.

According to this heresy, there is in the body a spiritual intelligence. As occasions arise this intelligence readily discriminates likes and dislikes and pros and cons, feels pain and irritation, and experiences suffering and pleasure—it is all owing to this spiritual intelligence. But when the body perishes, this spiritual intelligence separates from the body and is reborn in another place. While it seems to perish here, it has life elsewhere, and thus is immutable and imperishable. Such is the standpoint of the Senika heresy.

But to learn this view and try to pass it off as the Buddha Dharma is more foolish than clutching a piece of broken roof tile supposing it to be a golden jewel. Nothing could compare with such a foolish, lamentable delusion. Hui-chung of the T'ang dynasty warned strongly against it. Is it not senseless to take this false view—that the mind abides and the form perishes—and equate it to the wondrous Dharma of the Buddhas; to think, while thus creating the fundamental cause of birth-and-death, that you are freed from birth-and-death? How deplorable! Just know it for a false, non-Buddhist view, and do not lend an ear to it.

I am compelled by the nature of the matter, and more by a sense of compassion, to try to deliver you from this false view. You must know that the Buddha Dharma preaches as a matter of course that body and mind are one and the same, that the essence and the form are not two. This is understood both in India and in China, so there can be no doubt about it. Need I add that the Buddhist doctrine of immutability teaches that all things are immutable, without any differentiation between body and mind. The Buddhist teaching of mutability states that all things are mutable, without any differentiation between essence and form. In view of this, how can anyone state that the body perishes and the mind abides? It would be contrary to the true Dharma.

Beyond this, you must also come to fully realize that birth-and-death is in and of itself nirvana. Buddhism never speaks of nirvana apart from birth-and-death. Indeed, when someone thinks that the mind, apart from the body, is immutable, not only does he mistake it for the Buddha-wisdom, which is free from birth-and-death, but the very mind that makes such a discrimination is not immutable, is in fact even then turning in birth-and-death. A hopeless situation, is it not?

You should ponder this deeply: since the Buddha Dharma has always maintained the oneness of body and mind, why, if the body is born and perishes, would the mind alone, separated from the body, not be born and die as well? If at one time body and mind were one, and at another time not one, the preachings of the Buddha would be empty and untrue. Moreover, in thinking that birth-and-death is something we should turn from, you make the mistake of rejecting the Buddha Dharma itself. You must guard against such thinking.

Understand that what Buddhists call the Buddhist doctrine of the mind-nature, the great and universal aspect encompassing all phenomena, embraces the entire universe, without differentiating between essence and form, or concerning itself with birth or death. There is nothing—enlightenment and nirvana included—that is not the mind-nature. All dharmas—the "myriad forms dense and close" of the universe—are alike in being this one Mind. All are included without exception. All those dharmas, which serve as "gates" or entrances to the Way, are the same one Mind. For a Buddhist to preach that there is no disparity between these dharma-gates indicates that he understands the mind-nature.

In this one Dharma [one Mind], how could there be any differentiation between body and mind, any separation of birth-and-death and nirvana? We are all originally children of the

Buddha, we should not listen to madmen who spout non-Buddhist views.

Question 11: Is it necessary for those who devote themselves to zazen to strictly observe the Buddhist precepts?

Answer 11: Observing precepts, pure conduct, is a standard of the Zen school, and a characteristic of Buddhas and patriarchs. However, those who have not yet received the precepts, and even those who break the precepts, are not deprived of the benefits that come from zazen.

Question 12: May those who engage in the practice of zazen combine it with the practices of mantra recitation and Tendai shikan?"

Answer 12: When I was in China and had occasion to ask the masters there about the true principle of the schools, they told me they had never heard of any of the patriarchs, those who have rightly transmitted the Buddha-seal throughout the past in India and China, engaging in such combined practices. It is true. Unless you concentrate on one practice, you cannot attain the one [true] wisdom.

Question 13: Can lay men and women engage in this practice? Or is it limited to priests alone?

Answer 13: The patriarchs teach that when it comes to grasping the Buddha Dharma, no distinction must be drawn between man and woman, high and low.

Question 14: Upon entering the priesthood a person immediately sheds the various ties to secular life so there will *be nothing to hinder him in his negotiation of the Way in zazen. But how amid the pressures of secular life can he devote himself single-mindedly to such practice and bring oneself into accord with the Buddha Way that is beyond human agency?*

Answer 14: Buddha-patriarchs, moved by their great sense of pity for sentient beings, keep the vast gates of compassion open wide. They do this because they want to bring all living beings to realization. There is not a single being, either in the realm of the devas or among mankind, unable to enter. Throughout history we find much evidence to substantiate this. To mention just a few examples: Emperors Tai-tsung and Shun-tsung, though heavily burdened with the myriad affairs of state, negotiated the Way in zazen and penetrated to an understanding of the great Way of the Buddhas and patriarchs.

As imperial counselors serving at the emperor's side, Prime Ministers Li and Fang negotiated the Way in zazen and also realized the great Way. It is simply a question of whether the aspiration is there or not. It has nothing to do with whether one is a layman or a priest. What is more, those who are able to discern the true merits of things come to have faith in the Buddha Dharma naturally. Perhaps I should add that those who think mundane affairs hinder the practice of the Buddha Dharma know only that there is no Buddha Dharma in their daily life; they do not yet know that there is nothing "mundane" in the Buddha Dharma.

A recent minister of the Sung, named Feng, is another high official who excelled in the Way of the patriarchs. In a verse he composed late in his life, he wrote: "When free from my duties, I practice zazen, Rarely do I even lie down for sleep. I may appear to be a minister of state, but everyone calls me the "elder monk."

Although he could have had little time to spare from the duties of his office, he was possessed of a strong aspiration in the Way, and he attained realization. So you should consider your own situation in the light of others. Look at the present with an eye to the past.

Today in the land of the great Sung, the emperor and his ministers, those in official positions and ordinary citizens as well, men and women alike, everyone has the Way of the patriarchs constantly in their thoughts. Both soldiers and men of learning aspire to the study and practice of Zen. Many of those who so resolve are certain to awaken to an understanding of the mind-ground. Thus you can readily see that worldly affairs are no hindrance to the Buddha Dharma.

When the authentic Buddha Dharma spreads and is at work throughout a country, it is under the constant protection of the Buddhas and devas. Hence the benevolent rule of the king will be felt by his subjects, and the country will be at peace. Under a benevolent reign, with the country at peace, the influence of the Buddha Dharma is bound to increase.

Moreover, in the time of Gautama Buddha, even transgressors against the Dharma and those holding false views attained the Buddha Way. Among the followers of the Zen patriarchs, there were hunters and fuel-gatherers who attained satori, so is it possible that others would be unable to? But you must seek the guidance of an authentic teacher.

Question 15: Is it possible to attain realization by practicing zazen in this evil, degenerate age of the latter day?

Answer 15: While the doctrinal schools make much of names and forms, in authentic Mahayana teaching there is no differentiation between right, semblance, and final Dharma. It preaches that all who practice attain the Way. In fact, in the right Dharma that has been passed down without deviation, you enjoy the precious treasure within your own home the same upon entering it as a beginner as you do when you attain deliverance. Those who practice are themselves aware of their attainment or non-attainment, just as a person knows without any doubt whether the water he is using is warm or cold.

Question 16: Some say that if you penetrate fully the meaning of "the mind in itself is Buddha," even though you do not recite scriptures or actually engage in religious practice, you are lacking nothing of the Buddha Dharma. The mere knowledge that the Buddha Dharma inheres within you is the perfect, total attainment of the Way. You should not seek it elsewhere, in any other person. Then what need is there to trouble yourself with negotiating the Way in zazen?

Answer 16: Such words are especially meaningless. Were things as you portray them, would not all spiritually perceptive persons be able to arrive at understanding merely by being taught such words?

Understand that the Buddha Dharma consists above all in practice that strives to eliminate views that distinguish self and other. Were the Way attained by knowing your self is Buddha, Shakyamuni would not have troubled himself as he did long ago to lead others to enlightenment. Let me corroborate this with some examples of worthy priests of the past.

A monk of former times named Hsüan-tse was temple steward in the brotherhood of Zen master Fa-yen.[4] Fa-yen said to him, "Tse, how long is it that you've been with me?" "It's been three years now," he answered. "As a member of the next generation, why is it you never ask me about the Buddha Dharma?" Tse replied, "I must not deceive you. Formerly, when I was with Zen master Ch'ing-feng, I attained the Dharma realm of blissful peace." Fa-yen asked, "By what words did you attain that realm?" Tse replied, "I once asked Ch'ing-feng, 'What is the self of a Buddhist disciple?' He answered, 'Ping-ting t'ung-tzu comes for fire.'" "Those are fine words," said Fa-yen. "But you probably didn't understand them." Tse said, "I understand them to mean this: Ping- ting is associated with fire. To look for fire with fire is like looking for the self with the self." "You see," said the master, "you didn't understand. If that were the extent of the Buddha Dharma, it would not have been transmitted to the present day."

Hsüan-tse, indignant, promptly left the monastery. As he was leaving, he reflected, "The master is known throughout the land. He is a great teacher with over 500 disciples. There must be some merit in his admonishment."

He returned penitently to the monastery, performed his bows before Fa-yen, and asked, "What is the self of a Buddhist disciple?" "Ping-ting t'ung-tzu comes for fire," the master

---

4 Fa-yen Wen-i, 885-958, founder of the Fa-yen house of Chinese Zen. Hsüsan-tse was an heir of Fa-yen.

replied. On hearing these words, Hsüan-tse attained great enlightenment.

It is obvious the Buddha Dharma cannot be realized by understanding that "the self is the Buddha." If that were the extent of the Buddha Dharma, the master would not have said what he did to guide Hsüan-tse. He would not have admonished him as he did.

When you encounter a good master for the first time, just inquire about the rules and regulations with regard to practice, and then devote yourself wholeheartedly to negotiating the Way in zazen. Do not let your mind dwell upon superficial or partial knowledge. If you follow this advice, you will not find the Buddha Dharma's wonderful means unavailing.

Question 17: In scanning the past and the present in India and China one person was enlightened upon hearing a pebble strike against a bamboo; another's mind was cleared at the sight of blossoming flowers. Indeed, Shakyamuni himself realized the Way when he saw the morning star; and Ananda discerned the truth when a banner-pole fell. From the time of the Sixth Patriarch, a great many other people filiated to the Five Houses of Zen were enlightened by a single word or phrase. Yet did all of those people, to a man, negotiate the Way in zazen?

Answer 17: It should be clearly understood that those of the past and the present whose minds were enlightened by seeing things or hearing things all negotiated the Way without any preconceptions whatever; and that for each of them, right at that instant, no "other person" existed.

Question 18: In India and China people possess a natural intelligence and uprightness. When people in these centers of culture are taught the Buddha Dharma they are unusually quick to reach understanding and realization. In our country, however, benevolence and wisdom have not existed in abundance. It has been difficult for the right seeds to accumulate. It is indeed regrettable that our backwardness has produced this state of affairs. The priests in our country are inferior to even the laymen in those great lands. A general obtuseness pervades our entire culture, and the minds of our countrymen are small and narrow. People are deeply attached to worldly, material gain, partial to goodness and virtue of a very superficial kind. Even were such people to engage in the practice of zazen, would it really be possible for them to realize the Buddha Dharma?

Answer 18: As you say, benevolence and wisdom are still not widespread among our countrymen. Their dispositions are narrow and perverse. Even if the right Dharma, undistorted, were given to them, its ambrosial nectar would likely turn to poison. They are easily moved to seek fame and profit, and so they find it difficult to free themselves from attachment and illusion.

All that is true, and yet in entering into realization of the Buddha Dharma, the ordinary commonsense knowledge of men and devas is not necessarily the vehicle by which the world of illusion is transcended. Even in the Buddha's time, one man realized the four stages to sainthood because of a bouncing ball. The great Way was illuminated for another when she put on a surplice (kesa). Both were ignorant, dull-witted people, no more enlightened than beasts, but by virtue of right faith the path of deliverance from illusion opened for them. A laywoman experienced satori while watching a foolish old monk sitting silently as she was serving his meal. It was not the result of wisdom or of culture, and it did not depend upon the spoken word or upon the relating of a story. It was right faith alone that saved her.

Moreover, the spread of Shakyamuni's teaching through the 3,000 world universe took only about 2,000 years. The lands making up this universe are diverse. Not all of them are countries of benevolence and wisdom. Certainly their inhabitants are not all astute and sagacious. Yet the Tathagata's right Dharma is originally endowed with the strength of incomprehensibly great merit and virtue. When the time comes, the Dharma will spread in a land. If people just practice with right faith, they will all attain the Way, irrespective of the amount of intelligence they possess. Do not think because ours is not a land of great benevolence and wisdom, or because the people's knowledge is small and their understanding feeble, that the Buddha's Dharma cannot be comprehended here. Besides, the right seed of prajna-wisdom exists in abundance in all people. It seems only that, having rarely been in accord with that wisdom, our countrymen have as yet been unable to enjoy its use.

[EPILOGUE]

The foregoing exchange of questions and answers is not altogether consistent. The standpoints of questioner and replier have sometimes interchanged. How many flowers have been made to blossom in the sky! But in Japan the essential principles of negotiating the Way in zazen have not yet been transmitted. We must pity those who aspire to know them. Therefore, I have collected something of what I saw and heard while I was in China. I have written down the true secrets of the enlightened masters I encountered there so that I could convey them to practicers who might desire to know them. At this time I have not had occasion to go beyond this and describe the standards of behavior in their monasteries, or the rules and regulations I observed in their temples. Such matters do not lend themselves to hurried or casual exposition.

It is true that Japan is a remote land, lying beyond the clouds and smoke to the east of the Dragon Seas. Yet from the time of the Emperors Kimmei and Yômei, we have been blessed by the gradual west-to-east movement of the Buddha Dharma. However, a disorderly proliferation of doctrinal names and forms and ritual matters has taken place, and there have been difficulties regarding the place of practice as well.

Now as you fashion a hermitage among blue cliffs and white rocks and with mended bowl and tattered robe begin your religious discipline on your own by properly sitting in zazen, the matter transcending Buddha is immediately manifested, and the great matter of a lifetime of practice is forthwith penetrated to ultimate fulfillment. This is the instruction left by Lung-ya, and the style of the teaching bequeathed by Mahakashyapa. The manner and principles of the zazen you practice should be based on the Fukanzazengi, which I compiled during the preceding Karoku period.

Although the spread of the Buddha Dharma in a country should await the decree of the king, we need only remember the meaning of the message the Buddha delivered on Vulture Peak to recall that the kings, nobles, ministers, and generals presently ruling innumerable lands throughout the world all humbly received that message and were reborn in their present existence without forgetting the deep desire from their previous existence to protect and maintain the Buddha Dharma. Are not all the regions in which their influence prevails Buddha lands? So it does not necessarily follow that in order to propagate the Way of the Buddha-patriarchs, you must choose a favorable place and wait for ideal circumstances to develop. And you must never think that you are starting new from today.

That is why I have gathered these words together to leave for the wise ones who aspire to the true Dharma, as well as for those true practicers who seek the Way like floating clouds and drifting water-plants.

Bendōwa

Commentary

Striking Emptiness

Buddha-tathagatas all have a wonderful means, unexcelled and free from human agency, for transmitting the wondrous Dharma and realizing supreme and complete awakening.

The terms "Buddha" and "tathagata" are virtually interchangeable. "Buddha" means "awakened one," a person who has realized their true nature, and "tathagata" means "one who has come from suchness," which is essentially the same thing. Throughout Dogen's work, we find that he uses duplicates and words with very similar meanings juxtaposed for emphasis or stylistic flourish.

The key word in this sentence is "means," and Dogen speaks about it in exalted terms. "Means" is something that is used to reach or to achieve a goal, and in this case, it's the means that the enlightened masters use for the realization of one's true nature and transmitting the

Dharma, which are the teachings of the Buddha.[5] This "means" is none other than seated meditation or zazen. "Za" in Japanese means seated or sitting, and "zen" means meditation. This is not a "means to an end" in and of itself; that is to say, apart from the end result. In our case, this "means" – this zazen – is itself the manifestation of our true nature, so it is not only a means but also simultaneously the realization we seek. This "means" is what Dogen referred to in his first essay, *Fukanzazengi,*[6] as "practice-realization," where practice is realization and realization is practice.

It's intriguing to observe that the *Fukanzazengi,* being Dogen's first work upon returning to Japan, is dedicated to the practice of zazen. Roughly four years later, Dogen wrote his second work, once more emphasizing the significance of zazen. Dogen considers zazen unparalleled, describing it as "free from human agency," a phrase often rendered as "nothing further to do" or "beyond study and without intention." In essence, there is nothing further to pursue. According to Dogen, this practice serves as the gateway to realizing one's true nature and experiencing supreme and complete awakening.

————————————

[5] "Dharma" with a capital "D" refers to the teachings of the Buddha. A small "d" refers to all phenomena, the myriad objects of our perception, as in the phrase "the ten thousand dharmas."

[6] See Gallagher, *Meeting the True Dragon: Zen Master Dogen's Fukanzazengi.*

That this means is only passed directly from Buddha to Buddha without deviation is due to the jijuyu samadhi, which is its touchstone.

Jijuyu samadi refers to the quality of concentration achieved during zazen and is often translated as "self-fulfilling concentration" or "self-receiving and employing concentration." *Samadi* is a Sanskrit word that is common in Hindu, Buddhist and Yogic traditions, signifying a state of concentration or heightened awareness in meditation. Sometimes the Japanese word *zanmai* is used instead of the Sanskrit word *samadi*. *Jijuyu* comprises three characters: *ji*, meaning "oneself" or "self;" *ju*, meaning "to receive;" and *yu*, meaning "to use" or "to employ." Essentially, we are simultaneously receiving and using this samadhi or concentration. When we are just sitting, we are simply being, casting away our normal subject-object paradigm. In doing so, thoughts about yesterday or tomorrow fade away. The stories we tell ourselves, the thoughts constructed into sentences framed within the context of the future or the past, are recognized as abstract concepts of our discursive mind. In this moment, we simply are, devoid of a subject-object relationship. At this moment, both giving and receiving are dropped, and pure being is revealed. The one giving is the same as the one receiving, and vice versa. This "one" is not opposed to another "one" that is neither giving nor receiving. From this perspective, giving and receiving are one; there is just this one. This is the Great One beyond duality and our habitual subject-object dichotomy, which is why this samadi, or concentration, is called "self-fulfilling" or "self-receiving." In the Soto School of Zen today, the most common term used to refer to this is *shikantaza*, often translated as "just sitting." While lacking the precision of *Jijuyu samadhi* and its meaning of "self-fulfilling concentration" or "self-receiving and employing concentration," both terms embody casting away both subject and object to reveal the inexpressible heart of practice. At their core, they are one and the same, and this core is "its touchstone," sometimes translated as "its standard" or "essence" — that by which the Dharma is transmitted from Buddha to Buddha, from one awakened person to another. However, fundamentally speaking, there is nothing to pass from one person to another. The moment that we embody this *Jijuyu samadhi,* all has been transmitted.

To disport oneself freely in this samadhi, the right entrance is proper sitting in zazen.

"To disport oneself freely" simply means to enjoy the self-fulfillment of both receiving and giving in this concentration. "The right entrance" means the way to do that, and Dogen states that the way to enjoy this samadhi is through proper zazen. Dogen's advocacy for sitting meditation (zazen) is not what we find in the other prominent schools of Buddhism at the time, namely Tendai and Shingon, which emphasized ceremonies and the recitation of sutras. During his training at Kennin temple in Kyoto under Myozen, zazen was not the only practice being taught. In Japan at the time, Zen practice was relatively new, and it was therefore combined with other, more well-established schools of Buddhism such as Tendai and Shingon. Eisai,[7] who had brought Zen to Japan, built Kennin temple in 1202 to practice Zen meditation exclusively but was coerced by the Shogun in power at the time, Minamoto Yoriie, to include ceremonies and ritual practices of both the Tendai and Shingon schools.[8]

The Dharma is amply present in every person, but without practice, it is not manifested; without realization, it is not attained.

Previously, we established that the term "Dharma" signifies the teachings of the Buddha. However, the core of the Dharma lies in enlightenment. Enlightenment can be approached from various angles or points of view depending on its manifestation or our perception, and that is what Dogen is doing here. It's important to acknowledge that when we speak of an "experience" of enlightenment, we are, to some extent, constrained by language. Typically, an experience involves a subject perceiving an object or an action. However, in the context of enlightenment, there is no separate subject to undergo any particular experience, yet enlightenment unfolds.

---

[7] Myōan Eisai 1141 - 1215.

[8] To this day, a Shingon ceremony is still performed at Kennin-ji. See Dumoulin, p. 141.

In this passage, Dogen illuminates three fundamental aspects of the Dharma.[9] Despite their apparent distinctiveness, they essentially describe one entity. One could liken it to three different jewelers examining the same diamond, each inspecting it from a different facet. Examining a diamond from different facets will reveal different impurities and nuances of color. While their observations and descriptions may vary, they are all observing the same diamond. Similarly, Dogen presents enlightenment from three distinct perspectives.

To begin, we encounter the intrinsic aspect of enlightenment, as Dogen states, "The Dharma is amply present in every person." This idea is echoed at the start of the *Fukanzazengi*: "The Way is basically perfect and all pervading." Here, "basically" signifies the fundamental nature, our true nature; at its core, the Way pervades everywhere and is "perfect" not in the sense of flawlessness but in the sense that it cannot be otherwise. This eternal moment is all there is — ever was, or ever will be — pervading everywhere; there is nowhere it is not.

This intrinsic aspect expresses our fundamental enlightenment – the enlightenment inherent in all beings, whether animate or inanimate, and the entire universe. We and all things are enlightened. Dogen elsewhere calls it *genjokoan*, or the "full manifestation of ultimate reality."

---

[9] Dogen refers to three perspectives, however, it's important to note that each perspective functions as a sort of umbrella term encompassing other perspectives.

Despite its lofty wording, it simply refers to this present moment. When we hear or read that we are already enlightened, it points to this intrinsic aspect. It has been said that we practice zazen not to attain enlightenment, but because we are already enlightened. In other words, our practice reflects our inherent understanding of our innate enlightenment. It refers to this intrinsic aspect that each of us, without exception, embodies. Even the term "embodies" fails to convey the intimacy – we are not separate from this intrinsic nature; it's not something we possess that could be taken away. Fundamentally, it is who we are.

This is what the Buddha realized under the Bodhi Tree over 2,600 years ago. He declared, "I, all beings, the great earth, are the wisdom and virtue of the awakened one to thusness." The Buddha, upon awakening, recognized that all things were already enlightened. He didn't attain enlightenment; he simply realized that he was already enlightened. He immediately grasped this intrinsic enlightenment – not just his own, but that of all beings and all things, visible and invisible. This is precisely what Dogen meant when he said "The Dharma is amply present in every person."

Dogen now addresses the second aspect of enlightenment, which is practice: "But without practice, it is not manifest." The second aspect of enlightenment that Dogen elaborates on is what he terms "practice-enlightenment." Dogen emphasizes that the practice of meditation is not merely a means to an end – that is, a way to become enlightened – but rather, it is the very manifestation of our enlightened nature. This enlightened nature is the intrinsic enlightenment we were just discussing. This second aspect of enlightenment is the embodiment of the first intrinsic aspect. In other words, it is the actualization of our intrinsic enlightened nature. Proper sitting in meditation is, in itself, enlightenment, and is, therefore, practiced for no other reason than that alone.

Dogen refers to this practice as *jijuyu samadi*, which, as we have seen, is not merely sitting on a cushion and daydreaming about lunch or past interactions. It involves wholeheartedly being present on the cushion, embodying whatever unfolds in that moment, and cultivating awareness of the present experience. This is a vast and spacious awareness that excludes nothing and seeks nothing, neither rejecting nor clinging to whatever appears. In that moment, that which arises in our sphere of consciousness and the awareness of whatever is arising, are not two. In other words, our awareness, and the sensory objects appearing and disappearing within the realm of that awareness, are fundamentally one.

This is a spacious, self-reflexive and reciprocal awareness that remains non-reactive and non-judgmental. There is no separation between perceiver and perceived; it's just what is, without any distinction: a bird singing outside the window, the distant sounds of an airplane or a passing car, the sensation of our legs on the mat, the fragrance of incense, and the interplay of light and shadow on the floor in front of us. Without hindrance or grasping, we simply are whatever arises. It's not that we experience these things; rather, we are these things. We don't merely hear the crow's call from the treetop; we are the crow's call. We are the light on the floor, the scent of incense, and the thoughts passing through our mind. We are not only aware of all these phenomena but also aware that we are aware of this awareness. This is practice-enlightenment — the actualization of our true nature. It is what Dogen meant when he said, "without practice, it is not manifest."

But our practice doesn't stop there. Dogen goes on to say, "without realization, it is not attained." Realization refers to awakening or enlightenment — the immediate recognition of our true and authentic nature. This is a sudden shift from the realm of multiplicity to the realm of oneness, where we see that everything is interconnected, that everything is one and not two. Space and time dissolve. In Japanese, it is referred to as *kensho,* and for great enlightenment, it is called *daikensho. Kensho* literally means "seeing one's true nature or character." Attainment, however, is an ongoing, lifelong practice of deepening our understanding and integrating our realization into daily activities. Integration means living in harmony with — and embodying — our realization moment to moment. This embodiment involves being one with our realization and manifesting it in daily life. This attainment — sometimes referred to as actualization — involves clarifying our understanding through many years of practice and, sometimes, the examination of several hundred koans.[10] However, for this attainment to occur, there must be realization. Therefore, we must practice. It is for this reason that Dogen puts so much emphasis on zazen. Dogen calls zazen the "Dharma gate of repose and bliss."[11] Zazen is the manifestation of our innate enlightened nature, which we can realize in this lifetime. Without this realization, there can be no attainment.

It is not a question of one or many; let loose of it and it fills your hands. It is not bounded vertically or horizontally; speak it and it fills your mouth.

It's not a matter of whether it's one or two; it's neither. It's a oneness beyond the concepts of one or two. If there is no duality, how can there be oneness? Yet, our daily experience is inherently dualistic, while ultimately, it's all one. Any attempt to grasp this understanding slips through our fingers. Regardless of the depth and clarity of our awakening, clinging to it ultimately proves futile. We might yearn to relive the bliss and joy experienced in the aftermath of awakening, but holding onto those emotions only leads to disappointment, anger and resentment. Why? Because living in a state of perpetual bliss is unattainable; we are human beings, complex organisms wired by our senses to perceive the world through a subject-object narrative. Thus, we must let go. In other words, whatever realization we attain, we

---

[10] Koan practice is more often encountered in the Rinzai school of Zen as opposed to the Soto school.

[11] Dogen, "Fukanzazengi." See Gallagher p. 14.

simply let it be without grasping it or attempting to cultivate it. We consciously relinquish our hold on it, and in doing so it fills us even in the midst of what we might describe as its absence. This is what it means to release it from our grasp. Paradoxically, when we do, we realize it's still present. It doesn't go anywhere because it didn't arrive from anywhere. It has always been here. This is what Dogen refers to when he writes about it filling our hands.

Within this Dharma, Buddhas dwell everlastingly, leaving no perceptions in any sphere or direction; all living beings use it unceasingly, with no sphere or direction appearing in their perceptions.

We could say that all Buddhas are sentient beings; in other words, all awakened ones are human. This awakening is not limited by a beginning or by an end; there are simply those who realize they are awakened — and are thus awakened — and those who have not yet realized that they are awakened. Even those who have not yet realized their true nature are constantly using it unceasingly. It's always right here whether we realize it or not.

The negotiation of the Way with concentrated effort that I now teach makes myriad dharmas exist in realization and, in transcending realization, practices a total reality. Then, when you are over the barrier, with all bonds cast off, you are no longer affected by such segmented distinctions."

What does it mean to "transcend realization" and practice a "total reality?" Dogen doesn't merely guide his students to awaken to their true nature; realization, for him, is not enough — nor should it be for us, either. Upon awakening to our true nature, we transition from the realm of multiplicity to the realm of oneness — from the relative world of subject-object duality to the absolute world of non-duality. Regardless of whether the opening is shallow or deep, it has the potential to be a powerful turning point in our lives, revealing another perspective previously grasped only intellectually or conceptually. This profound shift can be likened to free-falling from an airplane for the first time. No matter how many books we read or videos we watch, the actual experience is incomparable to any idea we may have of it. The first time it happens is astonishing — so much so that we may never want it to end. The freedom, joy, bliss, and free-flowing sense of life is so intoxicating that we'll do almost anything to maintain them. We simply want to remain there. This awakening to the absolute is the joy of all joys, the bliss of all blisses, and a high like no other. Finally, we think, we've arrived home to where we truly belong.

However, as humans, we navigate the realms of work, relationships, and associated responsibilities — essentially, we live our lives with all their inherent baggage. Furthermore, persistent so-called negative emotions, such as anger, jealousy, greed, impatience, and sadness, may now irritate us more than ever. The relative world stubbornly endures. Once again, we find ourselves burdened by old habits, feelings, emotions, and trigger mechanisms that seem impossible to shed. In zazen, we seek solace in the spaciousness where no-thought abides — a vast and clear emptiness that now intimately resonates with us. This vast space entices us and draws us in, becoming a refuge from the burdens of everyday life and the persistence of our negative emotions. Immersed in zazen, we cling to our enlightenment like a life preserver in a sea of relativity from which we've long sought escape.

This realization, whether shallow or profound, must be transcended. To achieve a greater awakening, we must surpass, go beyond, and see through our initial insight. What does that mean precisely? We need to see through our awakening, allowing it to dissolve just as the relative did. In other words, we must discern the true nature of our enlightenment — an enlightenment beyond our initial awakening, not progressing from the relative to the absolute, but rather from the absolute to nothingness. This is crucial because of our unconscious tendency to exchange one reality for another, inadvertently solidifying our awakening into an object, like a lucky coin we keep in our pocket. Though the relative endures, we merely tolerate it because our overwhelming preference lies with the absolute. We mistakenly believe that we have arrived at our destination when, in fact, we are hopelessly lost.

At this point, the absolute needs to fall away, just as the relative did. The ground on which we stand must disappear so that we naturally cease the struggle of trying to approach life exclusively from the perspective of the absolute. The absolute must be seen as empty, mirroring our perception of the emptiness of the relative. When this occurs, the absolute will have been transcended, and at that moment, we clearly see the folly in our efforts to cling to it. With this realization, a newfound appreciation for the relative is revealed, and we will effortlessly no longer hold a preference for the absolute. We now truly perceive both the relative and the absolute as empty, enabling us to practice, as Dogen calls it, a "total reality." This is what is meant by being "over the barrier" and having "all bonds cast off." Not being affected by distinctions such as "relative" and "absolute" means not only awakening to our true nature but also seeing through our own enlightenment. Without a clear recognition of the emptiness of the absolute, we risk finding ourselves ensnared in a trap, having merely exchanged one solidified reality for another.

After having seen through our realization, we find ourselves liberated to embrace and appreciate the relative. This is the essence of "make myriad dharmas exist in realization." These myriad dharmas refer to the countless phenomena that populate our sensory experience, constituting the fabric of our perceived universe. In essence, it is the same relative reality we once sought to transcend through our spiritual practice. However, by transcending our realization, we come to embrace this relative reality rather than seek to escape it. By doing so, we go beyond the limitations of our initial realization, attaining a profound freedom that allows us to fully immerse ourselves in the totality of existence, embracing every aspect of our lives.

After the religious mind arose in me, awakening the desire to seek the Way, I visited many religious teachers throughout the country. I chanced to encounter the priest Myozen of Kennin-ji. Swiftly passed the frosts and flowers of the nine years I studied with him. During that time I learned something of the manner of the Rinzai school. As the chief disciple of the patriarch Eisai, it was Myozen alone who genuinely transmitted the supreme Buddha Dharma. None of Eisai's other followers could compare with him.

Dogen's religious awakening is said to have occurred at the tender age of seven, following the death of his mother. It was during her memorial service when young Dogen observed the rising smoke from an incense stick, that he had a profound awakening to the world of impermanence. By the age of 12, Dogen found himself residing at Enryakuji temple on Mount Hiei, where he underwent ordination in the Tendai school of Buddhism.

Dogen later encountered priest Myozen. Butsuju Myozen (1184 - 1225), a Japanese Zen teacher and successor of Myoan Eisai (1141 - 1215), became a pivotal figure in Dogen's life. Eisai, who had brought the Rinzai lineage from China, played a crucial role in establishing Rinzai Zen in Japan. Dogen studied under Myozen for nine years until Myozen's passing in 1225. This "chance encounter" likely occurred around 1214, and greatly influencing dogen's Zen practice. For one thing, he studied koans and received transmission from Myozen. Secondly, it was Myozen who brought him to China.

After that, I proceeded to great Sung China, where I visited leading priests of the Liang-che region and learned of the characteristics of the Five Zen Gates. Finally, I practiced under Zen master Ju-ching at Mount T'ai-pai, and there I resolved the one great matter of Zen practice for my entire life. Then, when I returned home, in the first year of the She-ting period of the Sung [1228], my thoughts immediately turned to preaching the Dharma for the salvation of my fellow beings — it was as though I had taken a heavy burden upon my shoulders. Nevertheless, in order to await the time when I can work vigorously to this end and unburden myself of the desire to spread the Dharma far and wide, I am for the time being living like a cloud or water plant, drifting without any fixed abode, attempting to transmit through my actions the way of life followed by outstanding Zen masters of the past.

In 1223, Dogen and other monks traveled from Japan to China with their teacher Myozen. They visited several monasteries until reaching Mount T'ai-pai and Tiantong monastery, led by the formidable Zen master Rujing (1162-1228).[12] Rujing was known as a strict disciplinarian who emphasized sitting meditation above all else. He told Dogen:

---

[12] Rujing is the Japanese spelling of Ju-ching. My Zen education, such as it is, has been entirely through the Japanese spelling of Chinese masters and I have retained that here.

Cross-legged sitting is the Dharma of ancient buddhas. Practicing meditation is dropping off body and mind. Offering incense, doing prostrations, chanting Nembutsu, repentance and reading sutras are not essential; in just sitting it is fully accomplished.[13]

Dogen "resolved the one great matter of Zen practice" in 1223, late at night when he heard Rujing admonishing a sleeping monk: "When you study under a master, you must drop body and mind! What's the use of single-minded intense sleeping!" The moment Dogen heard "Drop body mind," he experienced realization, and all his questions and doubts were resolved.[14]

Dogen's teacher Myozen died soon after their arrival at Tiantong monastery, and Dogen subsequently decided to remain there. Dogen stayed with Rujing for an additional two years, clarifying his understanding before returning to Japan in 1227 and, ultimately, to Kennin temple. One of the first things that Dogen did upon his return was to inter the remains of Myozen, and then he wrote a short essay entitled "Fukanzazengi."[15] It was during this period in 1231 that Dogen, living like "a cloud or water plant," wrote "Bendowa." He had, by then, already left

---

[13] Leighton, p. 386.

[14] Loori, "Dropping Off Body and Mind."

[15] See Gallagher, *Meeting the True Dragon.*

Kennin temple in 1230 and was temporarily living in a small temple called Anyoin near Fukakusa.

But there will be those who have no concern for gain or glory, authentic religious seekers whose desire for the Way takes precedence over all else. They will be led vainly astray by mistaken teachers, and the right understanding will be arbitrarily obscured from them. They will become needlessly drunk with their own delusions and immersed forever in the world of illusion. How can the true seed of prajna *be expected to quicken and grow within such seekers? How will they ever reach the moment of attainment? As I am now committed to a wandering life, to what mountain or river can they proceed to find me? It is a sense of pity for the plight of such people that now makes me write down for those who would learn to practice the Way, the customs and standards of the Zen monasteries of great Sung China that I saw with [my] own eyes and have learned and the profound teachings of their masters that I have succeeded to and follow and transmit. I want such seekers to know the right Buddha Dharma. Here are its true essentials.*

In this paragraph, Dogen conveys a deep appreciation for the "customs and standards" upheld in Zen monasteries in China, particularly at Tiantong, where he underwent a two-year training period under Rujing. Dogen's emphasis was not on the mere recitation of sutras, chanting, or even the study of koans, but rather on the committed practice of wholehearted zazen. While ceremonies had their place, they did not take center stage under his watchful and compassionate guidance.

Dogen unequivocally addresses the potential pitfalls of misguided teachers leading sincere students astray or students succumbing to their own delusions on the path of attainment.

At an assembly on Vulture Peak, the great teacher Shakyamuni Buddha imparted to Mahakashyapa the Dharma that was subsequently transmitted from patriarch to patriarch down to Bodhidharma. Bodhidharma traveled to China and conveyed the Dharma to Hui-k'e, marking the initial transmission of the Buddha Dharma to eastern lands. It then made its way in direct, personal transmission to the Sixth Patriarch, Ta-chien. By that time, the genuine Buddha Dharma had beyond doubt spread extensively in China. It appeared there with its essence unaffected by any ramifying doctrinal accretions. The Sixth Patriarch had two superior disciples, Huai-jang of Nan-yüeh and Hsing-ssu of Ch'ing-ün. As possessors and transmitters of the Buddha-seal, they were masters for men and devas alike. Their two schools spread and branched into Five Houses: the Fa-yen, Kwei-yang, Ts'ao-tung, Yün-men and Lin-chi schools. At present in the great Sung, the Lin-chi school alone is found throughout the country. Although among these Five Houses there are differences to be found, they are all equally based on the one Buddha-mind seal.

Following the words, "I want such seekers to know the right Buddha-Dharma. Here are its true essentials," Dogen outlines the authentic essence of the buddha dharma for genuine seekers. Rather than delving into an esoteric treatise, he presents the concrete lineage of transmission, spanning from the Buddha down to his present day.

Scriptural writings were transmitted to China from the western lands during the Latter Han dynasty. They spread over the empire. But even in China, no determination was reached about which of the various teachings was superior. Following the arrival of Bodhidharma from the west, these entangling complications were cut away at their source, and the one Buddha Dharma, free from all impurity, began to spread. We must pray that this will take place in our country as well.

Zen is often portrayed as a teaching or practice that transcends words and letters. Despite the abundance of texts, sutras, and books in the Zen canon, the fundamental teaching remains unaltered by them. Bodhidharma, born in India in the early fifth century and passing away around 530, journeyed to China from India and showed little interest in scriptures or temples, as exemplified by his renowned encounter with Emperor Wu.[16] For Bodhidharma, the essence lay in the transmission of the mind seal — a transmission that went beyond words, letters or the construction of temples. This essence, discovered by Dogen at Tiantong monastery under the attentive guidance of Rujing, was what Dogen aspired to convey to others upon his return to Japan.

---

[16] Emperor Wu asked Bodhidharma, "What is the first principle of the holy teaching?" Bodhidharma replied, "Vast emptiness, nothing holy."

It is said that all the patriarchs and Buddhas who have maintained the Buddha Dharma have without question considered practice based upon proper sitting in jijuyu samadhi as the right path that led to their enlightenment. All those who have gained enlightenment in India and China have followed in this way of practice as well. It is a matter of rightly transmitting the wonderful means in personal encounter from master to disciple, and on the disciple's sustaining the true essence thus received.

Dogen emphasizes that, above all else, zazen is crucial in practice. However, the zazen to which Dogen refers goes beyond merely sitting on a cushion; it involves engaging in "proper sitting in jijuyu samadhi," which we examined earlier. Dogen alternatively refers to this as "practice realization." According to him, this practice plays a vital role in leading to awakening, although, as we will explore later, awakening is not solely dependent upon zazen. Dogen further underscores the significance of transmission from master to disciple, emphasizing that the disciple must uphold and pass on the authentic Dharma.

According to the authentic tradition of Buddhism, this personally and directly transmitted Buddha Dharma is the supreme of the supreme. From the first time you go before your master and receive his teaching, you no longer have need for incense-offerings, homage-paying, nembutsu, penance disciplines, or sutra reading. Just cast off your body and mind in the practice of zazen.

In Japan during that period, other schools of Buddhism held dominance, placing emphasis on practices such as chanting nembutsu, offering incense, and reading sutras, — common activities of the time. Even during Dogen's tenure at Kennin-ji, zazen was not the exclusive practice. It was Master Rujing in China who revealed to Dogen that proper sitting in zazen was the sole essential practice required. The phrase "casting off body and mind" directly originates from Master Rujing.

When even for a short period of time you sit properly in samadhi, imprinting the Buddha-seal in your three activities of deed, word and thought, then each and every thing throughout the dharma world is the Buddha-seal, and all space without exception is enlightenment. Accordingly, it makes Buddhatathagatas increase the Dharma-joy welling from their original source and renews the adornments of the Way of enlightenment. Then, when all classes of all beings in the ten directions of the universe — hell-dwellers, craving spirits, and animals; fighting demons, humans, and devas — being all together emancipation and reveal their original aspects, at that time all things together realize in themselves the true enlightenment of the Buddhas. Utilizing the Buddha-body and immediately leaping beyond the confines of this personal enlightenment, they sit erect beneath the kingly tree of enlightenment, turn simultaneously the great and utterly incomparable Dharma wheel, and expound the ultimate and profound prajna *free from all human agency.*

When we sit zazen properly, there exists nothing beyond our zazen, and there is no individual engaged in sitting.

This zazen permeates the entire universe. Sounds of breathing, various odors, and objects in our field of vision may manifest, yet, in contrast to our usual way of being, there is no inner commentary labeling them, nor are we daydreaming about the past or the future. It's akin to sitting with the sky overhead: clouds, birds, leaves, airplanes, the sun, or the moon may pass, but none of these things intrude on the sky, and none are deemed good or bad. This intimately embodies the essence of "all space without exception is enlightenment."

When we awaken to our true nature, we recognize that, while we may have attained enlightenment, others have not. However, we clearly understand that they possess the potential to awaken to their own true nature. We also perceive that our own enlightenment remains incomplete until all sentient beings awaken to their true nature. Despite this fact, and perhaps paradoxically, we now see that the awakening of one single person is simultaneously the awakening of the entire universe. Fundamentally, we grasp that others are essentially ourselves, and our awakening, profound as it may be, and as far reaching as it may be, is only partial as long as others remain unenlightened. This illustrates the phrase "leaping beyond the confines of this personal enlightenment." If our enlightenment is solely aimed at alleviating our own suffering, we paradoxically risk perpetuating suffering both in ourselves and in others. True liberation is inextricably connected to the emancipation of all beings, and despite our own awakening, we are not truly enlightened until everyone else is also enlightened. Therefore, we naturally serve and assist others in realizing their true nature. We begin by sharing our practice and insights with our companions on the path, turning the Dharma wheel "free from all human agency." In other words, we engage in this practice without concern for other human activities, having nothing else to do.

Since, moreover, these enlightened ones in their turn enter directly into the way of imperceptible mutual assistance, the person seated in zazen without fail casts off body and mind, severs all the heretofore disordered and defiled thoughts and views emanating from his discriminating consciousness, conforms totally with the genuine Buddha Dharma, and assists universally in performing Buddha-work far and wide, at each of the various places the Buddha-tathagatas teach, that are as infinitely numberless as the smallest atom particles — imparting universally the ki *transcending Buddha, vigorously promoting the Dharma* (ho) *transcending Buddha. Then, with land, trees and grasses, fence and wall, tile and pebble, and all the things in the ten directions performing the work of Buddhas, the persons who share in the benefits thus produced from this wind and water all are imparted unperceived the wonderful and incomprehensible teaching and guidance of the Buddhas, and all manifest their own immediate and familiar enlightenment close at hand. Since those receiving and employing this fire and water all turn round and round the Buddha-making activity of original enlightenment, those who dwell and converse with them also join with one another in possessing inexhaustible Buddha-virtue, spreading it ever wider, circulating the inexhaustible, unceasing, incomprehensible, and immeasurable Buddha Dharma inside and outside throughout the universe.*

Essentially, when we wholeheartedly embark on the Way and focus on proper practice, we receive immeasurable support from those who have preceded us. We are not solitary practitioners on this path; our presence and practice extend far beyond ourselves, reaching others across the planet, resonating throughout space and time — touching both the visible and the unseen, those nearby and those far away. Simultaneously, we are touched, supported and guided by those who have gone before us as well as those practicing at this very moment.

Yet such things are not mingled in the perceptions of the person sitting in zazen because, occurring in the stillness of samadhi beyond human agency or artifact, they are, directly and immediately, realization. If practice and realization were two different stages, as ordinary people consider them to be, they should perceive each other. Any such mingling with perceptions is not the mark of realization, for the mark of true realization is to be altogether beyond such illusion.

Our perceptions are essentially creations of the mind, derived from our senses. What we perceive is the result of our mind processing information from our vision, hearing, tasting, smelling, touching, and thinking. During proper zazen, the distinctions between inside and outside dissolve; we cease to perceive anything. In other words, we stop entertaining thoughts about the observed, dismissing the cognitive impulses of our analytical and rational mind. While this discursive mind has its time and place in our lives, zazen is not one of those moments. Zazen is a practice that Dogen describes as a moment "beyond human agency."

With the phrase "If practice and realization were two different stages," Dogen strongly emphasizes the inseparability of practice and realization, asserting that they are inherently one and the same. Proper sitting in zazen is realization itself; it is the embodiment of our innate understanding. As the saying goes, "we do not practice to become enlightened, we practice because we are already enlightened." While ordinary people may perceive meditation as a means to attain enlightenment, the truth is that we are inherently enlightened, even if we're not fully conscious of it. This perspective may seem contradictory to Dogen's earlier statement about zazen being the sole path to awakening, but that context specifically addressed other religious practices like sutra recitation, chanting, offering incense, and nembutsu.

"They would perceive each other": Practice and realization are inseparable; hence, there is no perception of either one. If they were distinct entities, we could scrutinize, evaluate, or describe one in relation to the other. Since they are not separate, there is nothing to see, hear, taste, touch, smell or think about. Through embodying practice and realization, we immediately embody all things across the universe and beyond. This expresses the essence of what Dogen means by stating that practice and realization are not two.

"Any such mingling with perceptions is not the mark of realization": Discussions about practice and realization, while possible, amount to little more than the mind engaging in analysis and discursive thought. This mental activity, essential for survival, becomes mere idle distraction in the realm of realization. All perceptions are creations of our mind, and realization transcends the mind itself, which cannot even conceive of it. Therefore, any "mingling" of perceptions is merely the activity of the discursive mind.

Moreover, although both the mind of the person seated in zazen and its environment enter realization and leave realization within the stillness of samadhi, as it occurs in the sphere of jijuyu, *it does not disturb a single mote of dust, or obstruct a single phenomenon, but performs great and wide-ranging Buddha-work and carries on the exceedingly profound, recondite activities of preaching and enlightening. The trees, grasses, and land involved in this all emit a bright and shining light, preaching the profound and incomprehensible Dharma; and it is endless. Trees and grasses, wall and fence expound and exalt the Dharma for the sake of ordinary people, sages, and all living beings. Ordinary people, sages, and all living beings in turn preach and exalt the Dharma for the sake of trees, grasses, wall and fence. The realm of self-enlightenment* qua *enlightening others is originally filled with the characteristics of realization with no lack whatsoever, and the ways of realization continue on unceasingly.*

Dogen reveals the fluidity of the absolute and the relative when he speaks of entering and leaving realization "within the stillness of samadhi," shifting from a solidified to a fluid perspective, in what he often terms "practice-enlightenment." Seated, proper zazen performs profound Buddha-work, and involves sharing the Dharma and enlightening others. Within this practice-enlightenment awakening, all things — seen and unseen, including the trees, grasses, and land — preach an incomprehensible Dharma. This Dharma eludes understanding by our analytical, rational, and discursive mind; it is beyond comprehension. Yet, it can be experienced—not in the sense of an individual experiencing something, but rather, experience itself manifesting without a subject-object observer. Right here, this is just this — whatever "this" is. It's beginningless and endless. Why? Because it never commenced. There's no end and no beginning; how could there be a beginning? There is no end. "Trees and grasses, wall and fence expound and exalt the Dharma for the sake of ordinary people, sages, and all living beings". Yes, all of this, entering our perceptions, is nothing but the teaching of the Buddha. Centuries before, Rinzai expressed a similar sentiment: "The six-rayed divine light never ceases to shine."[17] These six rays of divine light represent our seeing, hearing, touching smelling, tasting and thinking. The Way is ever-present, throughout both day night. Wherever we go, this is always here. To realize this is to be a buddha, an awakened one. To merely understand it intellectually, to hold an idea or a concept in our minds, is, as Rinzai says, to be "born in the wombs of asses or cows." Everything around us exalts the

---

[17] Rinzai p. 8.

Dharma, and we, too, exalt the Dharma for the sake of all others. "The ways of realization continue on unceasingly." How could they not? Life itself is realization and never ceases, perpetuating infinitely in realms and in ways beyond our imagination. It unfolds and transmits endlessly, extending past forever and even far beyond.

Because of this, when just one person does zazen even one time, he becomes, imperceptibly, one with each and all of the myriad things and permeates completely all time, so that within the limitless universe, throughout past, future, and present, he is performing the eternal and ceaseless work of guiding beings to enlightenment. It is, for each and every thing, one and the same undifferentiated practice, one and the same undifferentiated realization. Only this is not limited to practice of sitting alone: the sound that issues from the striking of emptiness is an endless and wondrous voice that resounds before and after the fall of the hammer. And this is not limited to the side of the practicer alone. Each and every thing is, in its original aspect, endowed with original practice—it cannot be measured or comprehended. You must understand that even if all the numberless Buddhas in the ten directions, as countless as the sands of the Ganges, mustered all their might together and by means of Buddha-wisdom attempted to measure and totally know the merit of the zazen of a single person, they could not know the whole of its measure.

Do not mistakenly think that our meditation is an isolated event confined to the boundaries of time and space. As we sit in meditation, simply being and allowing thoughts and emotions to pass like clouds in the sky, we embrace everything — seen and unseen — throughout the known universe and beyond. When we sit in meditation, the windows themselves are sitting in meditation. With each inhalation, the lightbulbs draw breath too. The sound of a crow is our own voice calling amidst the rustling leaves.

This seamless, imperceptible reality constitutes all there is, and it is, in fact, our very true nature. In zazen, we engage in "performing the eternal and ceaseless work of guiding beings to enlightenment." Our zazen resonates with others in ways far beyond our imagination. It embodies the subtlest and purest expression of our innate kindness, compassion, and authentic, limitless nature.

Dogen emphasizes that this is, for each and every one of us, "the same undifferentiated practice" and "the same undifferentiated realization." There aren't two practices, nor are there two realizations. Although this is the same realization, our depth of realization may vary greatly from one person to another. In many ways, realization is comparable to a foreign country; if you've resided there and immersed yourself in the foreign culture, you likely know it quite well. Later, when encountering another person who has similarly lived and immersed themselves in the same culture, the intimacy of that shared connection is immediately apparent. However, there are those who have only briefly visited the country or merely glimpsed images of it in books or film. This understanding differs greatly from that of someone who has lived there. Nonetheless, it remains just one practice — just one realization — regardless of the depth of understanding.

"Only this is not limited to practice of sitting alone," reminds me of what Dogen previously wrote in the *Fukanzazengi*, "Zazen has nothing whatsoever to do with sitting or lying down."[18] Zazen encompasses all activities when performed selflessly. Practice and realization complete long before a practitioner sits down and crosses their legs, remaining so long after they rise from the cushion. The question is not about the existence or non-existence of realization; it doesn't come into being, nor does it disappear. It simply is — unaffected by whether anyone is engaged in sitting zazen or not.

Dogen writes: "The sound that issues from the striking of emptiness is an endless and wondrous voice that resounds before and after the fall of the hammer." The paradox of hearing a sound before the hammer strikes arises from hearing the sound independent of the hammer's action. While we typically perceive it only when the hammer falls, the sound in this case transcends the temporal confines of its creation. To illustrate, envision a completely cloudy sky. Suddenly, the clouds part, unveiling a patch of blue — truly remarkable indeed! Yet, the blue sky was not suddenly created; it had existed prior to the clouds parting and it being revealed. Similarly, the sound of the falling hammer exists before the strike. As well, our innate true nature is always

----

18 See Gallagher p. 13.

present, even if we are unaware of it — this is our "endless and wondrous voice," which is none other than our most precious gift.

Similarly, enlightenment doesn't come into being through any means. It doesn't manifest through effort on our part, nor does it rely on any external force. The phrase "striking emptiness" may seem absurd, like a carpenter's hammer striking the air. Yet, this mirrors the inherent paradox of realization — not as an object that materializes and disappears, appearing and vanishing — rather, it is always present whether we are aware of it or not. Realization doesn't suddenly appear, nor does it bring us anything; instead, it resembles the vast blue sky that may be obscured by the clouds. This resounding, wondrous voice, this vast blue sky, has been present all along.

Dogen continues with: "And this is not limited to the side of the practitioner alone." Our innate enlightened nature, our awakened birthright, transcends all known boundaries and permeates every corner of existence. It is fundamentally present throughout the known and unknown universe, even within individuals we may dislike, disapprove of, or consider evil. They, too, share the same enlightened nature as we do.

Dogen continues, asserting that this innate enlightened nature cannot be measured or grasped because it transcends the capabilities of our discursive mind. Emphasizing that the merit of the zazen of a single person cannot be comprehended by all the innumerable Buddhas throughout space and time, he urges us not to assume that this merit is confined to benefiting the one seated on the cushion. It extends far beyond the confines of temporal and spatial limitations, reaching out to touch and guide all people towards the realization of their own innate awakened nature — forever present and fully realized. The impact of a single person's zazen extends far beyond the limitations of individual practice, proving more beneficial to the world than the collective anger of a million people. It resonates universally, unhindered by the constraints of space and time, nurturing others on the path of awakening.

[QUESTIONS AND ANSWERS]

Question 1: You have told us all about the sublime merits of zazen. But an ordinary person might ask you this: "There are many entrances to the Buddha Dharma. What is it that makes you advocate zazen alone?"

Answer 1: Because it is the right entrance to the Buddha Dharma.

See commentary to question 2.

Question 2: But why single out zazen alone as the right entrance?

Answer 2: The great teacher Shakyamuni Buddha rightly transmitted zazen as the wonderful means for attaining the Way; all the tathagatas of the three periods attain the Way through zazen as well — which is why they transmit it from one to another as the true entrance. Besides, zazen is how all patriarchs from India in the west to China in the east, have gained the Way. That is why I now teach it to men and devas as the right entrance.

Dogen unequivocally emphasizes seated mediation — zazen. He asserts that Shakyamuni Buddha and all great patriarchs throughout India and China attained the Way through zazen and this is the reason Dogen exclusively focuses on teaching it. In 13th-century Japan, the Zen school was in its infancy. However, Dogen himself regarded the practice of zazen as being outside the confines of any specific school. In fact, it was considered heretical during that time. Despite the dominance of Buddhist schools like Tendai and Shingon in Japan, Dogen perceived zazen as the genuine gateway to the Way — the path leading to the awakening of our true nature.[19]

Question 3: The reason you give, that zazen transmits the Tathagata's wonderful means, which you base upon evidence you trace to the patriarchal teachers, may well be correct — such matters are really beyond an ordinary person's ability to ascertain. For all that, however, surely one can reach enlightenment by reciting sutras and repeating the nembutsu.

---

[19] Dumoulin, p. 160.

How can you be certain that if you pass your time sitting idly in zazen, enlightenment will result?

Answer 3: When you characterize the unsurprisingly great Dharma and the samadhi of the Buddhas as merely "sitting idly," you are guilty of maligning the Great Vehicle. It is as profound an illusion as to declare there is no water when you are sitting in the midst of the ocean. Fortunately, the Buddhas are already seated firmly established in jijuyu samadhi. Does that not produce immense merit? It is a pity that your eyes are not opened yet, that intoxication still befogs your mind.

The realm of Buddhas is utterly incomprehensible, not to be reached by the workings of the mind. How could it ever be known to a man of disbelief or inferior intelligence? Only a person of great capacity and true faith is able to enter here. A person who does not believe, even if he is told about such a realm, will find it impossible to comprehend. Even on Vulture Peak, the Buddha told some in the assembly that they might leave. If right faith arises in your mind, you should practice under a master. If it does not, you should cease your efforts for the time being and reflect with regret that you have not been favored with Dharma benefits from the past.

Besides, what do you really know of the merits brought by such practices as sutra-recitation and nembutsu? It is utterly futile to imagine that merely moving your tongue or raising your voice has the merit of Buddha-work. Any attempt to equate those practices with the Buddha Dharma only makes it more remote. Moreover, when you open a sutra to read, it should be for the purpose of clarifying the teachings the Buddha set forth about the rules and regulations for practicing sudden and gradual enlightenment, to convince you that you will attain realization if you follow them. It is not done in order to waste yourself in useless speculation and discrimination, and to suppose that you are thereby gaining merit that will bring you to enlightenment. Intending to attain the Buddha Way by foolishly working your lips, repeating some words incessantly a thousand or ten thousand times, is like pointing the thills of a cart northward when you want to go south, or like trying to fit a square piece of wood into a round hole. To read the Buddha's words while still unaware of the way of practice is as worthless a pastime as perusing a medical prescription and overlooking to mix the compounds for it. If you merely raise your voice in endless recitation, you are in no way different from a frog in a spring field — although you croak from morning to nightfall, it will bring you no benefit at all. Such practices are difficult to relinquish for those who are deeply deluded by fame or profit — this because of the depth of their covetousness. Such people were to be found in ancient times; there is no reason they should not be around today. They deserve our special pity.

Only make no mistake about this: if a student working under the constant guidance of a clear-minded, truly enlightened teacher realizes his original mind and rightly transmits his Dharma, the wondrous Dharma of the Seven Buddhas is then fully manifested and fully maintained. There is no way for this to be known or even to be approached by a priest who merely studies words. So you should have done with all these uncertainties and illusions; instead, negotiate the Way in zazen under the guidance of a true teacher and gain complete realization of the Buddhas' jijuyu samadhi.

What's crucial to understand here is that Dogen dismisses the practices of reciting sutras and chanting "nembutsu," the name of the Buddha. According to Dogen, these activities are not valid paths to enlightenment; instead, he sees them as a futile endeavor for the sincere practitioner aspiring to awaken to their true nature. In 13th-century Japan, these practices were widely endorsed by the Tendai and Shingon schools of Buddhism, but Dogen ridicules them, likening those who engage in such practices to frogs croaking in a spring field — entirely useless for those earnestly seeking enlightenment.

For the sincere student, finding a true teacher is most important — someone who has realized their true nature and can effectively guide a student along the Way. This aligns with the advice Dogen offered in the *Fukanzazengi*: "Revere the person of complete attainment who is beyond all human agency."[20] Dogen asserts that a priest who merely recites words and phrases is like a parrot, lacking the genuine understanding needed to guide others on the path of spiritual awakening.

Question 4: The teachings that are transmitted today in our own Hokke and Kegon schools represent the ultimate Mahayana teaching. Not to mention the teachings of Shingon, which were transmitted personally by Vairochana Buddha to Vajrasattva — they have not been handed down from master to disciple without good reason. Centered in the sayings "the mind in itself is Buddha," and "this very mind attains

---

[20] Gallagher, p. 15.

Buddhahood," Shingon teaches that the genuine enlightenment of the Five Buddhas is attainable in a single sitting, without having to pass through long kalpas of religious practice. It could perhaps be termed the most sublime point the Buddha Dharma has yet reached. In view of that, What are the advantages of the practice you advocate that you advance it alone and ignore all these others?

During Dogen's era, the predominant schools of Buddhism in Japan were Hokke, Kegon, Shingon, and Tendai. Each of these schools had its distinctive rituals, involving the recitation of sutras, mantras, and the offering of incense. However, unlike the Rinzai school of Zen or Dogen's current emphasis on meditation, none of these schools placed a significant emphasis on meditation. Dogen exclusively prioritized zazen over all other practices.

The student is clearly perplexed about Dogen's dismissal of these traditional practices, considering that they have been passed down for several centuries from master to disciple.

Answer 4: Be well assured that for a Buddhist the issue is not to debate the superiority or inferiority of one teaching or another, or to establish their respective depths. All he needs to know is whether the practice is authentic or not. Men have flowed into the Way drawn by grasses and flowers, mountains and running water. They have received the lasting impression of the Buddha-seal by holding soil, rocks, sand, and pebbles. Indeed, its vast and great signature is imprinted on all the things in nature, and even then remains in great abundance. A single mote of dust suffices to turn the great Dharma wheel. Because of this, words like "the mind in itself is Buddha" are no more than the moon reflected on the water. The meaning of "sitting itself is attainment of Buddhahood" is a reflection in a mirror. Do not get caught up in skillfully turned words and phrases. In encouraging you now to practice the immediate realization of enlightenment, I am showing you the wondrous Way by which the Buddha-patriarchs transmit the Dharma from one to another. I do this in the hope that you will become real men of the Way.

While Dogen asserts that his purpose is not to engage in debates about the superiority of one practice over another, he clearly believes that authentic sitting in zazen surpasses any other form of practice, and he states this unequivocally. All dharmas (all things) are the Way — soil, rocks, sand, pebbles, and even a speck of dust. This encompasses all six sense perceptions.[21] The mention of the moon reflected in water and reflections in a mirror signifies that what is perceived is merely a representation of that which we seek and not the true Dharma. This reminds us of the well-known phrase, "a painted rice cake does not satisfy hunger."[22] Instead, Dogen emphasizes "the immediate realization of enlightenment," which relies on nothing whatsoever.

---

[21] This is similar to "The six-rayed divine light never ceases to shine." See Rinzai, p. 8.

[22] For more on the story of the painted rice cake, see Dogen, *Treasury of the True Dharma Eye*, p. 193.

Moreover, in receiving and transmitting the Buddha Dharma, it is absolutely essential to have as a teacher a person who is stamped with realization. Word-counting scholars will not do — that would be a case of the blind leading the blind. Today, all who follow the right transmission of the Buddha-patriarchs preserve and maintain the Buddha Dharma by following with reverence a clear-sighted master who has attained the Way and is in accord with realization. Because of that, the spirits of the realms of light and darkness come to him and take refuge; enlightened Arhats also seek him out to beg his teaching. None are excluded from acquiring the means of illuminating the mind-ground. This is something unheard of in other teachings. Followers of Buddha should simply learn the Buddha Dharma.

Dogen underscores the crucial importance of finding a good teacher, echoing his sentiments from the "Fukanzazengi."[23] In the contemporary West, Zen teachers are relatively common, especially since some of them are not lineage holders capable of transmitting the teaching, but rather self-appointed Zen teachers. Dogen advises seeking a "clear-sighted master who has attained the Way and is in accord with realization." Being in accord with our realization is an ongoing, life-long practice that occurs moment by moment. Realizing our true nature doesn't automatically make us immune to arrogance;[24] post-realization work requires daily attention and awareness. Living in accord with our

---

[23] Gallagher, p. 89, "Revere the person of complete attainment who is beyond all human agency."

[24] For more context on arrogance and realization, see Gallagher, p. 30-32.

realization, as Dogen says, means embodying it with our whole being. This is the actualization of the Buddha Way. The resonance experienced in the actualization of our realization becomes our one and only true compass. Our intuition of whether our words or actions are in harmony with our realization or not is our guiding light as to whether we are embodying our realization or simply indulging in our deeply ingrained mechanisms and reactions. And, as Dogen says, someone in accord with their realization attracts all sorts of spirits and Arhats,[25] without excluding anyone.

You should also know that basically we lack nothing of highest enlightenment. We are fully furnished with it at all times. But because we are unable to come to complete agreement with it, we learn to give rise to random intellection and, by chasing them, supposing them to be real, we stumble vainly in the midst of the great Way. From these mistaken views appear flowers in the air of various kinds: thoughts of a twelve-link chain of transmigration, realms of twenty-five forms of existence, notions of three vehicles, five vehicles, Buddha, no-Buddha — they are endless. You must not think that learning such notions is the proper path of Buddhist practice.

Lacking nothing of "highest enlightenment" refers to our innate awakened nature, our innate buddha nature, with which everyone is endowed from the very beginning. We are "fully furnished with it" at all times and are never without it. "Unable to come to complete agreement with it" means that we have not realized it in the sense that we

---

[25] One who has attained enlightenment.

have not embodied it, we have not made it manifest in our daily lives. It's not that we are arguing with it and disagreeing with it; it's simply that we are truly unaware of our innate enlightened nature, and therefore we foolishly seek solace in what our discursive mind has created in its stead. We become content with paintings of rice cakes and movies about foreign countries instead of wholeheartedly seeking out a real rice cake or making the voyage to a foreign land. Our mind creates thoughts and forms concepts, notions, and opinions, which is far easier than training ourselves to set our thoughts aside, as Dogen encourages us to do in the "Fukanzazengi."[26] We may, in fact, have had some sort of realization, but because we have not yet transcended that realization, we cling to it, and this clinging becomes a struggle for us. We continue the folly of grasping at one thing and pushing away another!

"Flowers in the air" refers to people with eye diseases and is used here to express what is imaginary and not real.[27] In other words, all the intellectual chatter of all the realms of existence, the different vehicles, and even notions of Buddha and no-Buddha are nothing more than concepts and distractions from right practice. Yet, more often than not, this is what fascinates us the most and occupies our time. Dogen, of course, is clear that for him, this is not the proper path of Buddhist practice.

---

[26] Gallagher, p. 13.

[27] Dogen, Eihei, *The Heart of Dogen's Shobogenzo*, p. 17, footnote 39.

But now, when you cast everything aside by single-mindedly performing zazen in exact accordance with the Buddha-seal, at that moment you outstep the confines of illusion and enlightenment, sentiment and calculation and, unbothered by alternatives of unenlightened and enlightened, you stroll at ease beyond the world of forms and regulations enjoying the function of great enlightenment. How can those enmeshed in the traps and snares of words and letters begin to measure up to you?

Casting everything aside and single-mindedly performing zazen is precisely the act of dropping off body and mind, as Dogen has so often encouraged us to do. The confines of illusion and enlightenment are the definitions that our discursive mind gives to this moment. We find ourselves confined in our illusion when we say things such as, "this is delusion" or "this is enlightenment," "this is how an enlightened person behaves," and "this is how a deluded person behaves." Dogen encourages us to transcend these limitations, to see through these delusions, to where we are no longer preoccupied with being deluded or enlightened, in the relative or the absolute. In fact, we shed these notions like a snake shedding its skin. This is what Dogen means by strolling at ease "beyond the world of forms and regulations."

Question 5: Samadhi is one of the three learnings. Dhyana is one of the six paramitas.[28] Both are learned by all Bodhisattvas from the beginning of their religious life and practiced irrespective of a person's mental capacity. The zazen you speak of would seem to be included in these categories. What grounds do you have for stating that the right Dharma of the Buddha is concentrated solely in zazen?

The question is, if meditation is one of the six paramitas leading to enlightenment, why has Dogen chosen it above the others as the correct path to enlightenment?

Answer 5: Your question arises because the incomparable truth of the right Dharma eye that is the Buddha's great and central concern has come to be called the "Zen sect." Bear this well in mind: the appellation "Zen sect" is found in China and the lands east of China; it was unknown in India. During the nine years that the great teacher Bodhidharma performed zazen facing a wall at the Shaolin monastery on Mount Sung, the priests and laymen of the time did not yet know the right Dharma of the Buddha. They said Bodhidharma was an Indian monk whose religion consisted of doing zazen. In generations after that all Buddhist patriarchs invariably devoted themselves to zazen. Unthinking people outside of the priesthood, observing this and not knowing the true circumstances, began to speak loosely of a "Zazen sect." At present, the word za has been dropped, and people speak of the Zen sect. The essence of

---

[28] The six "perfections" or *paramitas,* are practices which lead to the attainment of enlightenment: donation, precept-keeping, perseverance, assiduity, meditation, and wisdom.

the school is made clear throughout the recorded sayings of the Zen patriarchs. It is not to be equated with the samadhi or dhyana included among the six paramitas or three learnings.

Dogen subtly differentiates the meditation he advocates and the paramita of meditation. During his time, the so-called "Zen sect" was on the fringes of conventional Buddhist schools and practices. Bodhidharma, credited with bringing "the Zen sect" to China from India, sat facing a wall at Shaolin monastery for nine years. Dogen emphasizes that the zazen he teaches aligns with the Buddha's teaching, or Dharma, and should not be confused with the simple meditation of the six paramitas or the samadhi of the three learnings.

Never has there been anything unclear or ambiguous about it. The Buddha himself wanted this Dharma to be his legitimate transmission. Some among the deva multitude now present in the heavens actually witnessed the ceremony that took place many years ago during the assembly on Vulture Peak, when the Tathagata [the Buddha] entrusted his right Dharma eye, his wondrous mind of nirvana, to Mahakashyapa alone. So there is no reason for any doubt. Without ever ceasing or diminishing their efforts, those deva hosts devote themselves to protecting and maintaining the Buddha Dharma throughout all eternity.

Dogen aligns his zazen practice with the teachings of Bodhidharma, emphasizing the transmission of the "right Dharma eye" and the Buddha's "mind of nirvana." This alignment mirrors the transmission on

Vulture Peak between the Buddha and Mahakashyapa.[29] During this ceremony, devas were believed to be present, and in Dogen's era, they continued tirelessly to safeguard and uphold the Dharma. According to Dogen, awakening and correct practice are inseparable — they are one. The proper practice of zazen embodies our innate awakened nature, indivisible from the enlightenment we seek and the *"mind of nirvana"* transmitted from the Buddha to Mahakashyapa. This is not to be confused with the paramita of simple meditation practice, which may not emphasize its indivisible nature with awakening.

You should just know without any doubt or uncertainty whatever that this Dharma [zazen] is, in its entirety, the all-inclusive Way of the Buddha's Dharma. There is nothing else even to compare with it.

Dogen emphasizes the inseparable connection between the Buddha's teachings (the Dharma) and the proper practice of seated meditation (zazen.) He describes zazen as "the all inclusive Way of the Buddha's Dharma," embodying the very awakening we strive for. This aligns with what Dogen frequently refers to as "practice-enlightenment" — our innate enlightenment unveiled through zazen, which sets it apart from other forms of meditation or practice. In other words, zazen is not just a practice but is itself the embodiment of the enlightenment we seek. Therefore, while zazen serves as both the path to and the manifestation of our enlightened

---

[29] This story is the subject of the first koan in *The Record of Transmission of Light.*

nature, ongoing practice is essential for deepening our understanding and awakening to this reality, ultimately allowing us to realize it for ourselves.

Question 6: What grounds are there for Buddhists to emphasize Zen meditation and place so much weight on sitting alone among the four attitudes (moving, standing, sitting, lying)? To say this is the path to entering realization?

In other words, why does Dogen advocate sitting above all other physical postures?

Answer 6: It is not possible to exhaustively survey the way in which Buddhas, one after another from ages past, have practiced and entered realization. If you must have a reason, you should simply know that this is the way that Buddhists use. Further reasons are unnecessary. Haven't patriarchs extolled zazen as the "Dharma gate of repose and joy," because among the four bodily attitudes it is sitting that affords repose and joy? Remember, this is the way of practice employed not by one Buddha or two, but by all Buddhas and all patriarchs.

The proper seated posture in zazen aligns with the practice followed by all patriarchs, tracing back to the Buddha, and as such, "Further reasons are unnecessary."

Question 7: So those who have not yet realized the Buddha Dharma[30] can, by negotiating the Way in the practice of zazen, attain that realization. But what about those who have already

---

[30] "Having not yet realized the Buddha Dharma" means not yet having experienced enlightenment.

achieved realization — what can they expect to gain by doing zazen?

In essence, the questioner is asking what purpose might zazen serve after achieving enlightenment? What benefits can an enlightened individual derive from practicing seated meditation?

Answer 7: Proverbs caution against relating one's dreams to the foolish, or placing boat-poles in the hands of woodsmen. Nevertheless, I will try to explain matters once again.

Dogen implies that the foolish may not grasp the significance of one's dreams, just as someone who works in a forest might be perplexed by the utility of a boat pole, possibly resorting to using it for firewood. In other words, what he is about to convey may not be understood by the questioner; however, Dogen will attempt to explain nevertheless.

To think practice and realization are not one is a non-Buddhist view. In the Buddha Dharma,[31] practice and realization are one and the same. As your present practice is practice within realization, your initial negotiation of the Way is in itself the whole of original realization. That is why from the time you are instructed in the way of practice, you are told not to anticipate realization apart from practice. It is because practice points directly to original realization. As it is from the very first realization in practice, realization is endless. As it is the practice of realization, practice is beginningless. Hence both

----

[31] Buddha Dharma" here means the teachings of the Awakened One, Siddhartha Gautama.

Shakyamuni and Mahakashyapa were brought into the great functioning by practice within realization. Bodhidharma and patriarch Hui-neng were also drawn into the functioning by practice within realization. And it has been the same for all those who have maintained the Buddha's Dharma.

Dogen emphatically asserts the inseparability of practice and realization — they are essentially one, referred to as "practice-realization." It's important to clarify that this notion does not advocate actively practicing being enlightened, as if giving a directive saying, "You should practice being enlightened." Such an interpretation oversimplifies the profound and wondrous meaning of "practice-realization." The true essence of "practice-realization" transcends this idea, embodying the notion that practice and enlightenment are inherently one.

When we immerse ourselves in proper zazen practice, we embody that very moment in time. Practicing within realization signifies that the present moment is itself realization, and our very life is realization. Therefore, when we practice, we do so in the context of this moment in time, which is, in essence, realization itself. Apart from this moment, there is no realization.

Dogen asserts that we "are told not to anticipate realization apart from practice. It is because practice points directly to original realization." This "original realization" refers to our innate enlightened nature — our buddha nature, our awakened nature, our true nature. It is the reason why we practice in the first place.[32] Our practice not only points to this innate enlightened nature but is also the embodiment of that very nature. However, it's important to recognize that, despite saying "it points to" or is the "embodiment of," these are not two separate entities; the pointing and embodying are simply concessions to language.

"As it is from the very first realization in practice, realization is endless." This line has also been translated this way: "As it is always already the realization of practice, there is no end to realization."[33] From the very beginning, realization exists within the context of practice, just as practice is always within the context of realization. Both Practice and realization are endless and beginningless. It is simply this moment in time without a past, present, or future. Awakened ancestors, from Shakyamuni to Mahakashyapa, Bodhidharma to Hui-neng, practiced within this realization.

It is practice inseparable from the outset from realization, and since fortunately we [practicers] all transmit a portion of wondrous practice ourselves, even our negotiation of the Way as beginners obtains a portion of original realization at a ground that is utterly free of human agency. You should know that in order to keep from defiling this realization that is inseparable from practice Buddhas and patriarchs teach

---

[32] A wise one of old said, "We do not practice to become enlightened, we practice because we are already enlightened."

[33] See Hoshin and Daninen, *Bendowa: A Talk on Exerting the Way.*

unceasingly that we must not allow our practice to diminish. When we cast off the wondrous practice, original realization fills our hands ; when we transcend original realization, wondrous practice permeates our bodies.

Dogen emphasizes once again that practice and realization are inseparable — they are one. In practicing the Way, we engage in both receiving and transmitting this practice and realization. Transmitting the practice inherently involves transmitting the realization as well. The moment we correctly practice, realization is embodied, and both this realization and embodiment are transmitted beyond any "human agency," in other words, beyond any human activity. Dogen, in other writing, refers to this as "Jijuyu Zanmai," or self-receiving and employing samadhi. Through correct and wholehearted practice, we simultaneously practice and transmit realization throughout the entire universe.

Dogen speaks of not defiling our realization by ensuring that our practice does not diminish. Ultimately, however, realization cannot be defiled or diminished; it is whole beyond any possibility of diminishment or defilement. Yet, our discursive mind continually attempts to stay at the forefront of our experience, and if we allow our practice to diminish, our awareness will recede into the background, and we may lose our way. This is why it is crucial to practice diligently and wholeheartedly.

The phrase "When we cast off wondrous practice, original realization fills our hands" has also been translated as "throw away"[34] or "let go of"[35] wondrous practice. The moment we hold on to something, it becomes an object separate from us. By clinging to it, we may feel a sense of possession, fearing its loss if not tightly held. However, allowing the present to simply be, without judgement, attachment, or repulsion enables us to embody it. Allowing our realization, as it is, to simply be without any clinging or sense of possession, is to manifest our innate enlightened nature, which is none other than zazen, this moment, and this very life.

"When we transcend original realization, wondrous practice permeates our bodies." Transcending original realization means going beyond our enlightenment, allowing it to be without clinging to it. This is only possible when we recognize its true nature, which is devoid of any substance — just as our normal, habitual, discursive mind is devoid of any solidity. In other words, when we perceive the emptiness of the absolute as we do with the relative, we liberate ourselves from grasping or clinging to either. Recognizing the emptiness of both the relative and the absolute is the transcendence of our original realization, our innate enlightened nature. In fact, not only is it the transcendence of our innate enlightenment, it's also the transcendence of our realization, our experience of enlightenment. When this occurs, "wondrous practice" not only permeates our

---

[34] Hoshin and Daninen.

[35] Nearman, Hubert, trans. Shobogenzo, Shasta Abbey Press, Mount Shasta, California, 2007, p. 13.

bodies but also transcends and permeates the entire seen and unseen universe.

When we speak of emptiness, we refer to the absence of anything solid or defined. It is not about the emptiness of something with an inside or an outside, like a vessel or a container. It's the absence of anything to grasp or hold onto — infinite, without boundaries or limits. Our usual experience of the world is full of boundaries and defined objects, space, and time — the relative world of our experience. Emptiness is the absence of these distinctions. At its core, the aim of Zen is to experience this emptiness directly and to see through our relative existence to the infinite beyond. However, in doing so, we may inadvertently solidify this experience, and find ourselves preferring the infinite of the absolute over the definite of the relative. Identifying with the absolute, we might come to regard the relative with disdain, having spent years trying to see beyond it. True freedom is not achieved until we see through the absolute, recognizing its true emptiness, and transcending it. Only then can "wondrous practice permeate our bodies."

When I was in Sung China, everywhere I went I saw that the Zen monasteries were all built to include a special hall for zazen. Five hundred or 600 monks, sometimes even up to 2,000 monks, were housed in these halls and encouraged to devote themselves to zazen day and night. When I asked the head priests of these monasteries, teachers who transmit the authentic seal of the Buddha-mind, about the essence of the Buddha's Dharma, they told me that practice and realization are not two stages.

A dedicated hall for zazen, as encountered by Dogen in Sung China, was a rarity in Japan during his time, where Zen remained a fringe sect, often regarded as heretical. Dogen was profoundly impressed by the commitment to zazen at these monasteries. Once again, he emphasizes the inseparability of practice and realization.

For that reason, I urge not only those who come here to practice with me, but all high-minded seekers who aspire to the truth that is found in the Buddha Dharma—whether beginners or experienced practicers, wise sages or just ordinary people—to conform to the teachings of the Buddha-patriarchs, to follow the Way of the true masters, and negotiate the Way in zazen.

Dogen invites the reader to practice zazen and negotiate the Way as all true masters have done in the past.

Do you know the words of one of those patriarchs? "It is not that there is no practice or realization, only that we must not contaminate them [by attaching to them]." Another said: "Those who are able to see the Way, practice the Way." What you must understand is that your practice takes place within realization.

There is practice and there is realization, yet fundamentally, they are inseparable. However, practice and realization may be perceived as distinct entities. Becoming attached to our practice or realization is a transgression of our fundamental nature, which does not cling to or control anything. Contaminating our practice and realization occurs when we cling to them, turning them into objects. Not attaching to them simply means allowing our realization to be, as it is. In this way, we embody our practice and realization, preventing any transgression. "Those who are able to see the Way, practice the Way." We may not even be aware that we see the Way; we just find ourselves practicing the Way. However, if we are practicing the Way, we must, fundamentally, perceive it on some level. Our practice takes place within realization in the same way our realization takes place within practice. There is nothing but realization, and our practice is the embodiment of it.

Question 8: In former times, when teachers traveled to China and returned as Dharma-transmitters to spread Buddhism in our country, why did they ignore zazen and transmit only the doctrines?

Answer 8: Teachers in the past did not transmit zazen because the circumstances were not yet ripe for it.

Buddhism arrived in Japan in the 6th century but the practice of seated meditation would take another few hundred years.

Question 9: Did the teachers of earlier times understand this Dharma (zazen)?

Answer 9: If they had, they would have made it known.

Question 10: Some have said: "Do not concern yourself about birth-and-death. There is a way to promptly rid yourself of birth-and-death. It is by grasping the reason for the eternal immutability of the 'mind-nature.' The gist of it is this: although once the body is born it proceeds inevitably to death, the mind-nature never perishes. Once you can realize that the mind-nature, which does not transmigrate in birth-and-death, exists in your own body, you make it your fundamental nature. Hence the body, being only a temporary form, dies here and is reborn there without end, yet the mind is immutable, unchanging throughout past, present, and future. To know this is to be free from birth-and-death. By realizing this truth, you put a final end to the transmigratory cycle in which you have been turning. When your body dies, you enter the ocean of the original nature. When you return to your origin in this ocean, you become endowed with the wondrous virtue of the Buddha-patriarchs. But even if you are able to grasp this in your present life, because your present physical existence embodies erroneous karma from prior lives, you are not the same as the sages.

"Those who fail to grasp this truth are destined to turn forever in the cycle of birth-and-death. What is necessary, then, is simply to know without delay the meaning of the mind-nature's immutability. What can you expect to gain from idling your entire life away in purposeless sitting?"

What do you think of this statement? Is it essentially in accord with the Way of the Buddhas and patriarchs?

The question essentially asks about a soul within the body that is separate from it and does not perish with the body but rather continues on elsewhere.

Answer 10: You have just expounded the view of the Senika heresy. It is certainly not the Buddha Dharma.

The Senika heresy existed at the time of the Buddha and Dogen explains it in his answer.

According to this heresy, there is in the body a spiritual intelligence. As occasions arise this intelligence readily discriminates likes and dislikes and pros and cons, feels pain and irritation, and experiences suffering and pleasure—it is all owing to this spiritual intelligence. But when the body perishes, this spiritual intelligence separates from the body and is reborn in another place. While it seems to perish here, it has life elsewhere, and thus is immutable and imperishable. Such is the standpoint of the Senika heresy.

Dogen lays out the foundational principles of the Senika heresy. In contemporary terms, some might refer to this as the belief in a soul transmigrating from the body upon death, being reborn in a different form or place.

But to learn this view and try to pass it off as the Buddha Dharma is more foolish than clutching a piece of broken roof tile supposing it to be a golden jewel. Nothing could compare with such a foolish, lamentable delusion. Hui-chung of the T'ang dynasty warned strongly against it. Is it not senseless to take this false view—that the mind abides and the form perishes—and equate it to the wondrous Dharma of the Buddhas; to think, while thus creating the fundamental cause of birth-and-death, that you are freed from birth-and-death? How deplorable! Just know it for a false, non-Buddhist view, and do not lend an ear to it.

In other words, Dogen says not to pay any attention to this theory.

I am compelled by the nature of the matter, and more by a sense of compassion, to try to deliver you from this false view. You must know that the Buddha Dharma preaches as a matter of course that body and mind are one and the same, that the essence and the form are not two. This is understood both in India and in China, so there can be no doubt about it. Need I add that the Buddhist doctrine of immutability teaches that all things are immutable, without any differentiation between body and mind. The Buddhist teaching of mutability states that all things are mutable, without any differentiation between essence and form. In view of this, how can anyone state that the body perishes and the mind abides? It would be contrary to the true Dharma.

From the perspective of the Dharma (the teachings of the Buddha), concepts of immutability and mutability are merely notions created by the mind. There is neither change nor lack of change. Body and mind are inseparable and not distinct. Both undergo death and decay, yet neither truly dies nor parishes.

Beyond this, you must also come to fully realize that birth-and-death is in and of itself nirvana. Buddhism never speaks of nirvana apart from birth-and-death. Indeed, when someone thinks that the mind, apart from the body, is immutable, not only does he mistake it for the Buddha-wisdom, which is free from birth-and-death, but the very mind that makes such a discrimination is not immutable, is in fact even then turning in birth-and-death. A hopeless situation, is it not?

Nirvana is not a distant destination; rather, it exists in this very moment, not waiting for us elsewhere. How could it exist apart from birth or death? It's none other than this right here, whatever this is.

You should ponder this deeply: since the Buddha Dharma has always maintained the oneness of body and mind, why, if the body is born and perishes, would the mind alone, separated from the body, not be born and die as well? If at one time body and mind were one, and at another time not one, the preachings of the Buddha would be empty and untrue. Moreover, in thinking that birth-and-death is something we should turn from, you make the mistake of rejecting the Buddha Dharma itself. You must guard against such thinking.

Dogen advocates for embracing the reality of birth-and-death, urging us not to turn away from its inevitable nature. Rejecting the actuality of this cycle can lead to fixation on the concept of a transmigrating soul within it — a perspective we must be mindful of and strive to avoid.

Understand that what Buddhists call the Buddhist doctrine of the mind-nature, the great and universal aspect encompassing all phenomena, embraces the entire universe, without differentiating between essence and form, or concerning itself with birth or death. There is nothing—enlightenment and nirvana included—that is not the mind-nature. All dharmas— the "myriad forms dense and close" of the universe—are alike in being this one Mind. All are included without exception. All those dharmas, which serve as "gates" or entrances to the Way, are the same one Mind. For a Buddhist to preach that there is no disparity between these dharma-gates indicates that he understands the mind-nature.

All things seen and unseen in the universe are one; this oneness is what Dogen refers to as the "mind-nature." It's not a oneness opposed to duality but an all-encompassing unity. Everything, including enlightenment and delusion, are this very oneness. The myriad phenomena, here referred to as dharmas, serve as gates or paths to the Way. What we see, hear taste, touch, smell, and even think are all paths to the Way — these are the gates. This very moment, whatever it may be, is a gate, which itself encompasses myriad gates. Even those feelings or emotions we wish to discard serve as gates — even anger is a gateway to non-duality. One who preaches this "understands the mind-nature."[36]

In this one Dharma [one Mind], how could there be any differentiation between body and mind, any separation of birth-and-death and nirvana? We are all originally children of the Buddha, we should not listen to madmen who spout non-Buddhist views.

The separation or differentiation between our physical body and our mind or spirit is impossible; enlightenment and this cycle of birth and death are inseparable. There is only this one, which is not opposed to duality.

Question 11: Is it necessary for those who devote themselves to zazen to strictly observe the Buddhist precepts?

Answer 11: Observing precepts, pure conduct, is a standard of the Zen school, and a characteristic of Buddhas and patriarchs.

---

[36] This is similar to Master Rinzai when he said, "The six-rayed divine light never ceases to shine." See Rinzai, p. 8.

However, those who have not yet received the precepts, and even those who break the precepts, are not deprived of the benefits that come from zazen.

Dogen once wrote, "When we do zazen, what precept is not being observed?"[37] The observance of precepts naturally follows our practice; it's not the other way around. We don't observe the precepts to improve our practice; rather, we practice, and in doing so, we embody the precepts. This doesn't negate the fact that following the precepts can contribute to minimizing suffering in the world and improving our relationships. Both observing the precepts and practicing zazen undoubtably yield beneficial effects not only for the practitioner but also for all sentient beings. However, when we truly see that zazen is the fundamental teaching of the Buddha, we realize how all other teachings emanate from this practice.

Question 12: May those who engage in the practice of zazen combine it with the practices of mantra recitation and Tendai shikan?"

Answer 12: When I was in China and had occasion to ask the masters there about the true principle of the schools, they told me they had never heard of any of the patriarchs, those who have rightly transmitted the Buddha-seal throughout the past in India and China, engaging in such combined practices. It is true. Unless you concentrate on one practice, you cannot attain the one [true] wisdom.

---

[37] Dogen, Eihei, *The Heart of Dogen's Shobogenzo*, p. 23, footnote 54.

The questioner is referring to the mantras and recitation of the Shingon school of Buddhism, as well as the meditation practices of the Tendai school, both of which were popular and widely practiced in Japan during Dogen's time. Dogen explicitly discourages the combination of practices from these different schools.

Question 13: Can laymen and women engage in this practice? Or is it limited to priests alone?

Answer 13: The patriarchs teach that when it comes to grasping the Buddha Dharma, no distinction must be drawn between man and woman, high and low.

Our innate awakened nature exists in both women and men, regardless of social status. With regards to the Dharma, there is no preferential treatment for those who choose the path of priests or monks; everyone is equal when it comes to the Dharma.

Question 14: Upon entering the priesthood a person immediately sheds the various ties to secular life so there will be nothing to hinder him in his negotiation of the Way in zazen. But how amid the pressures of secular life can he devote himself single-mindedly to such practice and bring oneself into accord with the Buddha Way that is beyond human agency?

Answer 14: Buddha-patriarchs, moved by their great sense of pity for sentient beings, keep the vast gates of compassion open wide. They do this because they want to bring all living beings to realization. There is not a single being, either in the realm of the devas or among mankind, unable to enter. Throughout history we find much evidence to substantiate this. To mention

just a few examples: Emperors Tai-tsung and Shun-tsung,
though heavily burdened with the myriad affairs of state,
negotiated the Way in zazen and penetrated to an
understanding of the great Way of the Buddhas and patriarchs.

The Way is open to all: monks, priests, and lay people
alike — there is no distinction. Both Tai-Tsung and Shun-
tsung were Tang Dynasty emperors and Zen
practitioners.

As imperial counselors serving at the emperor's side, Prime
Ministers Li and Fang negotiated the Way in zazen and also
realized the great Way. It is simply a question of whether the
aspiration is there or not. It has nothing to do with whether one
is a layman or a priest. What is more, those who are able to
discern the true merits of things come to have faith in the
Buddha Dharma naturally. Perhaps I should add that those
who think mundane affairs hinder the practice of the Buddha
Dharma know only that there is no Buddha Dharma in their
daily life; they do not yet know that there is nothing
"mundane" in the Buddha Dharma.

Regardless of whether we're ordained or not, the Way is
open to each and every one of us — man or woman,
young or old, brilliant or illiterate. The Way is always
there, accessible to all. "Those who can discern the true
merits of things" is sometimes translated as "those who
can discern good from bad or superior from inferior." In
other words, those who have a sense of what aligns them
more with the Way than not.

It's interesting to note that Dogen finds nothing "mundane" about daily human activity. Those who believe that the mundane and routine activities of our lives hinder our practice and negotiation of the Way do not yet realize that each aspect of our daily activity embodies nothing but the Buddha Dharma. Ultimately, there is nothing outside of the Way.

A recent minister of the Sung, named Feng, is another high official who excelled in the Way of the patriarchs. In a verse he composed late in his life, he wrote:

"When free from my duties, I practice zazen, Rarely do I even lie down for sleep. I may appear to be a minister of state, but everyone calls me the "elder monk."

Although he could have had little time to spare from the duties of his office, he was possessed of a strong aspiration in the Way, and he attained realization. So you should consider your own situation in the light of others. Look at the present with an eye to the past.

Regardless of our familial duties and work responsibilities, a strong aspiration for attaining the Way enables us to realize our true nature. This realization is independent of free time, work, or marital status — it depends upon absolutely nothing at all.

Today in the land of the great Sung, the emperor and his ministers, those in official positions and ordinary citizens as well, men and women alike, everyone has the Way of the patriarchs constantly in their thoughts. Both soldiers and men of learning aspire to the study and practice of Zen. Many of those who so resolve are certain to awaken to an understanding of the mind-ground. Thus you can readily see that worldly affairs are no hindrance to the Buddha Dharma.

Dogen explains that in Sung China, even the emperor, his ministers, others in official positions, and ordinary people, aspire to the Way. In doing so, many of them will, in effect, realize their true nature. Nothing stands in the way of anyone realizing their true nature. Hindrance — or lack thereof — is nothing but a concept of the mind.

When the authentic Buddha Dharma spreads and is at work throughout a country, it is under the constant protection of the Buddhas and devas. Hence the benevolent rule of the king will be felt by his subjects, and the country will be at peace. Under a benevolent reign, with the country at peace, the influence of the Buddha Dharma is bound to increase.

Moreover, in the time of Gautama Buddha, even transgressors against the Dharma and those holding false views attained the Buddha Way. Among the followers of the Zen patriarchs, there were hunters and fuel-gatherers who attained satori, so is it possible that others would be unable to? But you must seek the guidance of an authentic teacher.

There is nothing stopping us from realizing our true nature — not even transgressions against the Dharma or having false views. Nothing can stop it. Even ordinary people who have never heard of the Dharma may realize their true nature. However, Dogen once again implores us to find a teacher — and he specifies that it should be an authentic one.

Question 15: Is it possible to attain realization by practicing zazen in this evil, degenerate age of the latter day?

The question refers to a period following the Buddha's death — referred to as "the latter day." It was believed to be a time without authentic Buddhist teachers or practice.

Answer 15: While the doctrinal schools make much of names and forms, in authentic Mahayana teaching there is no differentiation between right, semblance, and final Dharma. It preaches that all who practice attain the Way. In fact, in the right Dharma that has been passed down without deviation, you enjoy the precious treasure within your own home the same upon entering it as a beginner as you do when you attain deliverance. Those who practice are themselves aware of their attainment or non-attainment, just as a person knows without any doubt whether the water he is using is warm or cold.

"Right, semblance, and final Dharma" refer to three periods following the Buddha's death. The first period, called the Right Dharma, lasted for 1,000 years, during which doctrine, practice, and enlightenment all coexisted. The second period, Semblance Dharma, also lasted for 1,000 years, during which doctrine and practice existed but not enlightenment. The third period, Final Dharma, would last for 10,000 years. During this time, neither practice nor enlightenment would exist; only the doctrine would remain. It was a period (and still is for some) of pessimism about one's ability to practice and attain enlightenment.[38]

Dogen makes it clear, however, that we are all endowed with innate enlightenment — this is the "precious treasure within your own home." This is our treasure and we realize it through practice. This realization is self-affirming in the sense that we instantly recognize it as such and know it when we encounter it, just as we immediately know whether water is warm or cold when we touch it; there is no doubt nor need for external confirmation.

Question 16: Some say that if you penetrate fully the meaning of "the mind in itself is Buddha," even though you do not recite scriptures or actually engage in religious practice, you are lacking nothing of the Buddha Dharma. The mere knowledge that the Buddha Dharma inheres within you is the perfect, total attainment of the Way. You should not seek it elsewhere, in any other person. Then what need is there to trouble yourself with negotiating the Way in zazen?

In essence, if we are inherently enlightened — perfect, whole, and complete as we are — why bother striving for something called "awakening" or "enlightenment?" Dogen addresses this rhetorical question in his essay "Fukanzazengi" when he asks, "It is never apart from one, right where one is. What's the use of going off here

---

[38] Dogen, Eihei, *The Heart of Dogen's Shobogenzo*, p. 25, footnote 60.

and there to practice?"[39] The underlying issue, as we will explore, lies in an intellectual or conceptual grasp of the Buddha Dharma. It's an understanding that we are Buddhas and innately enlightened, but it remains a conceptual understanding derived from reasoned deduction — a mere depiction of the proverbial rice cake.[40] Who, truly hungry, would be satisfied with an image of a rice cake?

Answer 16: Such words are especially meaningless. Were things as you portray them, would not all spiritually perceptive persons be able to arrive at understanding merely by being taught such words?

Exactly. If that were true, why bother with practice? We would simply need to study the words to arrive at the desired understanding. However, this is not the case.

Understand that the Buddha Dharma consists above all in practice that strives to eliminate views that distinguish self and other. Were the Way attained by knowing your self is Buddha, Shakyamuni would not have troubled himself as he did long ago to lead others to enlightenment. Let me corroborate this with some examples of worthy priests of the past.

Dogen refers to Shakyamuni Buddha, as he did when addressing this question in the "Fukanzazengi." The views that delineate self from other are continuously generated by the mind. The Buddha Dharma transcends

---

[39] Gallagher, p. 25.

[40] "A painting of a rice cake does not satisfy hunger."

these views, revealing an absolute oneness or unity of all things, both seen and unseen. The practice of zazen embodies this realization, where distinctions and thoughts are no longer cultivated by our attention.

A monk of former times named Hsüan-tse was temple steward in the brotherhood of Zen master Fa-yen.[41] *Fa-yen said to him, "Tse, how long is it that you've been with me?" "It's been three years now," he answered. "As a member of the next generation, why is it you never ask me about the Buddha Dharma?" Tse replied, "I must not deceive you. Formerly, when I was with Zen master Ch'ing-feng, I attained the Dharma realm of blissful peace." Fa-yen asked, "By what words did you attain that realm?" Tse replied, "I once asked Ch'ing-feng, 'What is the self of a Buddhist disciple?' He answered, 'Ping-ting t'ung-tzu comes for fire.'" "Those are fine words," said Fa-yen. "But you probably didn't understand them." Tse said, "I understand them to mean this: Ping- ting is associated with fire. To look for fire with fire is like looking for the self with the self." "You see," said the master, "you didn't understand. If that were the extent of the Buddha Dharma, it would not have been transmitted to the present day."*

Ping-ting t'ung-tzu (Japanese, hyojo doji) translates to "fire boy," signifying the personification of fire, as explained in the notes by Abe and Waddell for this translation. Tse argues that seeking fire with fire is like searching for the self with the self. However, this merely reflects a conceptual understanding. Fa-yen immediately

---

[41] Fa-yen Wen-i, 885-958, founder of the Fa-yen house of Chinese Zen. Hsüsan-tse was an heir of Fa-yen.

understands this and admonishes him without hesitation.

Hsüan-tse, indignant, promptly left the monastery. As he was leaving, he reflected, "The master is known throughout the land. He is a great teacher with over 500 disciples. There must be some merit in his admonishment."

His ego bruised, Tse packs his bags and prepares to leave, but something holds him back.

He returned penitently to the monastery, performed his bows before Fa-yen, and asked, "What is the self of a Buddhist disciple?" "Ping-ting t'ung-tzu comes for fire," the master replied. On hearing these words, Hsüan-tse attained great enlightenment.

How wonderful it is that Tse returned to the monastery and posed the same question to Fa-yen that he had previously asked his previous teacher, Ch'ing feng. In this moment, Tse is open to further exploration, seeking a deeper understanding than what he currently possesses. Fa-yen responds with the same answer, and at that instant, Tse experiences a profound realization. This realization transcends the mere intellectual comprehension of the words reiterated by Fa-yen.

It is obvious the Buddha Dharma cannot be realized by understanding that "the self is the Buddha." If that were the extent of the Buddha Dharma, the master would not have said what he did to guide Hsüan-tse. He would not have admonished him as he did.

Fa-yen would not have been hard on Tse if it were simply an intellectual matter.

When you encounter a good master for the first time, just inquire about the rules and regulations with regard to practice, and then devote yourself wholeheartedly to negotiating the Way in zazen. Do not let your mind dwell upon superficial or partial knowledge. If you follow this advice, you will not find the Buddha Dharma's wonderful means unavailing.

This is sage advice. When arriving at a Zen center or another place of practice, inquire about the rules. Obtain a copy of the schedule and keep it with you. Be punctual. Practice zazen wholeheartedly and cultivate that practice in all other aspects of your life.

"Do not let your mind dwell upon superficial or partial knowledge." A Zen master once said, "Do not be satisfied with paltry gains." Our minds will often be content with the most superficial understanding. When we think we have found something, we must not stop there; we must continue our inquiry more profoundly.

When we practice wholeheartedly, the entire universe comes to our aide. Masters of the past will manifest and guide us. We are never alone in practice.

Question 17: In scanning the past and the present in India and China one person was enlightened upon hearing a pebble strike against a bamboo; another's mind was cleared at the sight of blossoming flowers. Indeed, Shakyamuni himself realized the Way when he saw the morning star; and Ananda discerned the truth when a banner-pole fell. From the time of the Sixth

*Patriarch, a great many other people filiated to the Five Houses
of Zen were enlightened by a single word or phrase. Yet did all
of those people, to a man, negotiate the Way in zazen?*

The question is: Did these individuals negotiate the Way
in zazen? Did each of them exert themselves to realize
their true nature? Implicit in the question is the
assumption that each enlightenment experience
mentioned occurred without prior effort on the part of
the practitioner. Therefore, must we genuinely make an
effort in our journey along the Way?

*Answer 17: It should be clearly understood that those of the
past and the present whose minds were enlightened by seeing
things or hearing things all negotiated the Way without any
preconceptions whatever; and that for each of them, right at
that instant, no "other person" existed.*

Having no preconceptions means having no
preconceived notions about anything. In other words,
there are no concepts or beliefs in the mind
superimposed on the information delivered by the
senses. In that moment, there is nothing else except what
is present; therefore, as Dogen says, "no 'other' person
existed." There is no other. There is no one. There is no
person to experience awakening, realization or
enlightenment. Simply put, there is no one and no thing.
However, there is awakening, realization, and
enlightenment.

*Question 18: In India and China people possess a natural
intelligence and uprightness. When people in these centers of*

culture are taught the Buddha Dharma they are unusually quick to reach understanding and realization. In our country, however, benevolence and wisdom have not existed in abundance. It has been difficult for the right seeds to accumulate. It is indeed regrettable that our backwardness has produced this state of affairs. The priests in our country are inferior to even the laymen in those great lands. A general obtuseness pervades our entire culture, and the minds of our countrymen are small and narrow. People are deeply attached to worldly, material gain, partial to goodness and virtue of a very superficial kind. Even were such people to engage in the practice of zazen, would it really be possible for them to realize the Buddha Dharma?

It's likely that the denigrating opinions in this question about the Japanese belong to Dogen himself. Having practiced in China and observed the dedicated meditation halls (Zendos) and the sincerity of practice, Dogen desired to replicate this in Japan, where it didn't yet exist — at least not to his liking. Stating that the Buddhist priests in Japan were inferior to the laypeople of China and India must have been considered heresy at the time. How could Dogen himself assert this? How could he claim that the entire Japanese culture was obtuse, populated by people of small and narrow minds? Most likely, he would have faced repercussions, perhaps being summoned to the emperor's court and reprimanded.[42] However, by framing these views as a

----

42 This text was written after Dogen had left Kyoto because the Hiei priesthood was contemplating destroying Dogen's home and expelling him from the capitol. See the introduction.

question from another person, he could express them without being the direct author — even if he agrees with them in the answer.[43]

Answer 18: As you say, benevolence and wisdom are still not widespread among our countrymen. Their dispositions are narrow and perverse. Even if the right Dharma, undistorted, were given to them, its ambrosial nectar would likely turn to poison. They are easily moved to seek fame and profit, and so they find it difficult to free themselves from attachment and illusion.

Agreeing with the questioner, Dogen admonishes the Japanese, describing their dispositions as "narrow and perverse." His critique becomes particularly scathing when he suggests that the wonderful bounty (ambrosial nectar) of the Dharma would turn to poison. Even in the contemporary West, the desire for fame and profit is widespread, and this includes some Zen teachers as well. No one remains immune.

All that is true, and yet in entering into realization of the Buddha Dharma, the ordinary commonsense knowledge of men and devas is not necessarily the vehicle by which the world of illusion is transcended. Even in the Buddha's time, one man realized the four stages to sainthood because of a bouncing ball. The great Way was illuminated for another when she put on a surplice (kesa). Both were ignorant, dull-witted people, no

---

[43] This is a subtle yet important nuance. However, it may partially explain why this text disappeared and remained completely unknown for hundreds of years after Dogen's death.

more enlightened than beasts, but by virtue of right faith the path of deliverance from illusion opened for them. A laywoman experienced satori while watching a foolish old monk sitting silently as she was serving his meal. It was not the result of wisdom or of culture, and it did not depend upon the spoken word or upon the relating of a story. It was right faith alone that saved her.

The key word in the first sentence above, for me, is "yet." The truth of all that being said does not hinder awakening for anyone. Our personal views and understanding of the world do not prevent awakening from occurring. Dogen gives three examples of awakening brought about by a bouncing ball, putting on a kesa, and serving a meal. Awakening can happen anywhere, at anytime, to any person. Awakening to our true nature has nothing whatsoever to do with intelligence or culture. It doesn't depend on reading a text or reciting a sutra. It does not even depend upon thinking good thoughts or being pure of spirit — realization may even occur during a moment of anger. Dogen says that it was "right faith alone that saved her," yet I would say that realization doesn't even depend on that either. Our awakening depends on absolutely nothing at all. This is not to say that we are helpless in bringing this about. Proper sitting in zazen, counting our breath or working on koans, and working with a teacher are all important aspects of our negotiating the Way. However, whether we ultimately awaken to our true nature does not depend on any of these things. Wholehearted practice, sincerity of aspiration, and practicing with love are all indispensable aspects of negotiating the Way — yet realization is not dependent on any of them.

Moreover, the spread of Shakyamuni's teaching through the 3,000 world universe took only about 2,000 years. The lands making up this universe are diverse. Not all of them are countries of benevolence and wisdom. Certainly their inhabitants are not all astute and sagacious. Yet the Tathagata's right Dharma is originally endowed with the strength of incomprehensibly great merit and virtue. When the time comes, the Dharma will spread in a land. If people just practice with right faith, they will all attain the Way, irrespective of the amount of intelligence they possess. Do not think because ours is not a land of great benevolence and wisdom, or because the people's knowledge is small and their understanding feeble, that the Buddha's Dharma cannot be comprehended here. Besides, the right seed of prajna-wisdom exists in abundance in all people. It seems only that, having rarely been in accord with that wisdom, our countrymen have as yet been unable to enjoy its use.

When Dogen asserts that "the right seed of prajna-wisdom exists in abundance in all people," he is referring to our innate enlightened nature, our inherent buddha nature — the awakened essence within each of us without exception. Even those who may seem dull or unremarkable possess this innate enlightened nature. However, before we can bring our lives into harmony with this true nature, we must first become aware of it. It is this awareness of our innate buddha nature that nurtures faith in our capacity to realize it. While realization is not dependent on faith, cultivating faith in our inherent awakened nature creates a more fertile ground from which this buddha nature can be revealed.

[EPILOGUE]

The foregoing exchange of questions and answers is not altogether consistent. The standpoints of questioner and replier have sometimes interchanged. How many flowers have been made to blossom in the sky! But in Japan the essential principles of negotiating the Way in zazen have not yet been transmitted. We must pity those who aspire to know them. Therefore, I have collected something of what I saw and heard while I was in China. I have written down the true secrets of the enlightened masters I encountered there so that I could convey them to practicers who might desire to know them. At this time I have not had occasion to go beyond this and describe the standards of behavior in their monasteries, or the rules and regulations I observed in their temples. Such matters do not lend themselves to hurried or casual exposition.

The reason, of course, that the "standpoints of questioner and replier have sometimes interchanged" is likely because Dogen himself posed these questions to provide the responses. These eighteen questions likely represent a compilation of inquiries Dogen encountered upon his return to Japan, reformulated here to encompass the most common ones. Dogen emphasized that the essential means for "negotiating the Way" was zazen. While he didn't entirely dismiss practices like mantras, sutra recitation, and prayer, they weren't the primary focus of the practice he taught. Even Kenninji, the Zen temple where Dogen practiced with Myozen for nine years, had elements of Shingon Buddhism intertwined with meditation.[44] The "true secrets" Dogen refers to are found in the *Bendowa*, as well as in his previous work, *Fukanzazengi*.

It is true that Japan is a remote land, lying beyond the clouds and smoke to the east of the Dragon Seas. Yet from the time of the Emperors Kimmei and Yômei, we have been blessed by the gradual west-to-east movement of the Buddha Dharma. However, a disorderly proliferation of doctrinal names and forms and ritual matters has taken place, and there have been difficulties regarding the place of practice as well.

Both Kimmei and his son Yomei served as emperors of Japan in the 6th century. In 552, a Korean king presented Emperor Kimmei with a bronze image of Shakyamuni Buddha, along with sutras and religious objects. Buddhism didn't begin to flourish until Kimmei's son, Yomei, ascended to the throne in 585. When Dogen writes that "there have been difficulties regarding the place of practice as well," he is referring to his time in China, where he encountered buildings exclusively dedicated to the practice of zazen. In Japan, this was not the norm. In 1236, shortly after his return to Japan, Dogen constructed the first fully independent Zen temple with a

---

[44] See Dumoulin p. 157-8.

dedicated meditation hall. The only practice allowed in the meditation hall was zazen.[45]

Now as you fashion a hermitage among blue cliffs and white rocks and with mended bowl and tattered robe begin your religious discipline on your own by properly sitting in zazen, the matter transcending Buddha is immediately manifested, and the great matter of a lifetime of practice is forthwith penetrated to ultimate fulfillment. This is the instruction left by Lung-ya, and the style of the teaching bequeathed by Mahakashyapa. The manner and principles of the zazen you practice should be based on the Fukanzazengi, which I compiled during the preceding Karoku period.

Dogen advocates a life of poverty, symbolized by a mended bowl and a tattered robe. This aligns with the guidance imparted by Lung-ya, who emphasized, "Studying the Way is above all learning poverty. Study poverty, live in poverty, and immediately you are close to the Way."[46] Concerning the practice of zazen, Dogen directs the reader to his *Fukanzazengi* which was written a few years prior.

Although the spread of the Buddha Dharma in a country should await the decree of the king, we need only remember the meaning of the message the Buddha delivered on Vulture Peak to recall that the kings, nobles, ministers, and generals presently ruling innumerable lands throughout the world all

---

[45] Dumoulin, p. 157-8.

[46] Lung-ya Chu-tun 835-923. See Dogen, Eihei, *The Heart of Dogen's Shobogenzo*, footnote 72, p. 30.

humbly received that message and were reborn in their present
existence without forgetting the deep desire from their previous
existence to protect and maintain the Buddha Dharma. Are not
all the regions in which their influence prevails Buddha lands?
So it does not necessarily follow that in order to propagate the
Way of the Buddha-patriarchs, you must choose a favorable
place and wait for ideal circumstances to develop. And you
must never think that you are starting new from today.

First, Dogen respectfully acknowledges the power and
position of kings, nobles, ministers, and generals who
rule over vast lands worldwide. He suggests that the
spread of the buddha dharma should await the decree or
authorization of the rulers of those lands. However, he
points out that those same rulers were present ("humbly
received that message") on Vulture Peak when the
Buddha transmitted the teachings to Mahakashyapa.
They were then reborn during Dogen's era "without
forgetting the deep desire from their previous existence
to protect and maintain the Buddha Dharma."

In a way, Dogen is praising the current rulers while
subtly reminding them of their inherent desire to protect
and maintain the Buddha Dharma. All the lands over
which they preside are fertile "buddha lands," and these
lands are just as conducive to practice as any other.
Instead of waiting for the right time or moving to the
right place, Dogen encourages us to engage in practice
and teaching right where we are.

When we commence our practice and teaching, we
should not, for a moment, believe that we are starting

something entirely new or from scratch. Have faith that the practice and teaching we undertake are activities we have been engaged in for many lifetimes throughout our collective history.

That is why I have gathered these words together to leave for the wise ones who aspire to the true Dharma, as well as for those true practicers who seek the Way like floating clouds and drifting water-plants.

This essay, lost for over four centuries after Dogen's death, is indeed an inspiration to those who aspire to the "true Dharma." Seeking the way "like floating clouds and drifting water-plants" is reminiscent of Lung-ya Chu-tun, who once said, "If my contemporaries ask where I live, tell them the green waters and blue mountains are my home."[47]

---

[47] Dogen, Eihei, *The Heart of Dogen's Shobogenzo*, footnote 72, p. 30.

Works cited

Dogen, Eihei. *The Wholehearted Way*. Kosho Uchiyama, commentary. Shikoku Okumura and Taiga Daniel Leighton, translators. Tuttle Publishing, 1977.

Dogen, Eihei. "Dogen's Bendowa." Normal Waddell and Abe Masao, translators. "The Eastern Buddhist," New Series, Vol. 4, No. 1 (May, 1971), pp. 124-127.

Dogen, Eihei. "Fukanzazengi." Norman Waddell and Abe Masao, translators. "The Eastern Buddhist," New Series, Vol. 6, No. 2 (October, 1973), pp. 115-128.

Dogen, Eihei. *The Heart of Dogen's Shobogenzo*. Norman Waddell and Masao Abe, translators. State University of New York Press, 2002.

Dogen, Eihei. *Meeting the True Dragon: Zen Master Dogen's Fukanzazengi*. Daniel Gallagher, commentary. Norman Waddell and Abe Masao, translators. St. Georges Press, 2019.

Dogen, Eihei. *Treasury of the True Dharma Eye: Zen Master Dogen's Shobo Genzo*. Kazuaki Tanahashi, ed. Shambala Publications, 2010.

Dumoulin, Heinrich. *A History of Zen Buddhism*. Paul Peachey, translator. Pantheon Books, 1963.

Hoshin, Anna and Yasuda Deninen, translators. *Bendowa: A Talk on Exerting the Way*. Great Matter Publications, 2009.

Leighton, Taigen Dan, ed. *Dogen's Extensive Record: A Translation of the Eihei Koroku*. Taigen Dan Leighton and Shohaku Okumura, translators. Wisdom, 2010.

Loori, John Daido and Kazuaki Tanahashi, translators. *The True Dharma Eye: Zen Master Dogen's Three Hundred Koans*. Shambala, 2011.

Rinzai. *The Record of Linji*. Thomas Yahoo Kirchner, ed. Rather Fuller Sasaki, translator and commentary. 1975. University of Hawai'i Press, 2009.

About the Author

Daniel Kōjin Gallagher Sensei was born in Newton, Massachusetts, and is a successor of Dr. David Keizan Scott Roshi of the StoneWater Zen Center in Liverpool, England in the lineage of Taizan Maezumi Roshi. He began Zen practice in 1991 with a Burlington, Vermont affiliate of Zen Mountain Monastery as well as with Sunyana Graef Roshi of the Vermont Zen Center. He spent over two decades in France, working as an English teacher and translator. He trained for many years with Catherine Genno Pagès Roshi in Montreuil. He holds a BA and an MA from St. Michael's College in Vermont as well as masters' degrees and a doctorate in Comparative Literature from the Université de Paris III - Sorbonne Nouvelle. He is the author of *D'Ernest Hemingway à Henry Miller : Mythes et réalités des écrivains américains à Paris (1919 - 1939)* and *Meeting the True Dragon: Zen Master Dogen's Fukanzazengi*. For more information please visit www.stonewaterzen.org.

Made in the USA
Monee, IL
14 March 2025

13989755R00083